Retirement Planning From Z to A

"Build your retirement plan in two minutes, then improve it."

A book

By

Patrick Clermont

Library and Archives Canada Cataloguing in Publication

Clermont, Patrick, 1969-

A Book

ISBN 978-1-7776504-6-9

**THIS IS NOT INVESTMENT ADVICE
IT'S AN INVESTMENT STORY** (YOUR
STORY WILL BE DIFFERENT)

The content in this book is for informational purposes only, you should not construe any such information as legal, tax, investment, financial, or other advice. Nothing contained in this book constitutes a solicitation, recommendation, endorsement, or offer by the author.

All content in this book is information of a general nature and does not address the circumstances of any particular individual or entity. Nothing in this book constitutes professional and/or financial advice.

You alone assume the sole responsibility of evaluating the merits and risks associated with the use of any information within the pages of this book. Always seek professional advice before making any decisions based on such information or other Content.

You agree not to hold the author of this book liable for any possible claim for damages arising from any decision you make based on information or other content made available to you in this book.

There is always a risk when investing; this is why we strongly recommend that you seek professional financial advice before making any decisions on buying, selling, or investing in any way, shape or form.

Introduction

Throughout this book I use "I" and "We" interchangeably. Don't let it scare you. :) There is no way that any of this could have been possible without the encouragement, support and ideas from my wonderful wife.

Whether you like it or not you're on your way to retirement, be it good, bad or ugly. When you get there, you may find yourself in a comfortable situation or struggling to make ends meet. Some of you may have a plan, others not so much. You may be forty years away or forty days. Whatever may be the case, you're on your way.

Spoiler alert, this book will not fix your life nor will it bare the "secret" to all your hopes and dreams. What we're hoping is that it might help you see the road you're on and help you improve your final destination. This book is all about tiny steps and how each one can have a positive impact on your life.

We are all different. I'll remind you of that throughout this book. Although we're all distinct individuals we do tend to have some shared similarities. That being the case, over the last few years I've come to realize that the people I've met seem to fall into three motivational groups, they are: Money, Toys & Time.

Just to be clear these aren't the only things in life that motivate us. But financially speaking they have the most impact and since we're dealing with finances we are going to be using them as our "raison d'être". That said, I don't think that anyone is a hundred percent one type or another. For example I see myself as 75% Time, 20% Money and 5% Toys.

As we move forward you need to think about what motivates you. The sooner you figure it out the more power you'll have in making the right choices for improving your retirement plan. Think back to when you were a kid and the choices you made, then move on to your teens and adulthood, you will see a pattern I guarantee.

Before moving on I would like to mention that the "people, friends and acquaintances" I mention in this book are not actual individuals. Throughout my life I have questioned and listened to all kinds of people in all kinds of situations and circumstances. In the following pages I have mash up these "like-minded" mavericks into one type of person or another.

For example my "Money motivated character" is a medley of individuals some of which are dead. A few are in their seventies and others are as young as twenty. That being said, if you still think I'm writing about you specifically, I'm not. If after reading this book you still think I'm writing about you… please Google Carly Simon's song "You're so vain" and seek professional help.

1. Money

Group one's motto is "Life is a game and money is how we keep score." This crowd will never have enough money. It's not that they make it just to spend it and buy things; I mean they do spend and buy. But I have found that these money musterers simply enjoy generating revenue. They are driven to work hard and will likely do so until the day they die. On their deathbeds they claim they never worked a day in their lives. Warren Buffet is a great example of this. He's in his nineties, worth well over a hundred billion dollars and he still goes to work every day.

2. Toys

This circle's motto is "Life is a game and the one that dies with the most toys wins." This bunch will work and work and work, but it's not for the money. It's for what the money can buy. Trust me there is a difference. They have the cars, the boats, the TVs, the planes, the games, etc. This group likes to feel good and as it turns out buying stuff is one way to release the magical feel good chemical we call dopamine. Often it's not how much time they have to play with their toys, it's just having them.

3. Time

This collective's motto is "You can always make more money, but you can't make more time." This group likes to make enough money to cover their needs and some occasional wants. Some of these folks will wear a twenty year old pair of pants, if it means not having to work to buy a new pair. Autonomy is their greatest desire.

No group is better than the other. Although if you heard them talk about each other you'd think that each one thinks they're better than the next. Money thinks Time is lazy. Time thinks Toys is flushing money down the toilet. Toys thinks Money is a tightwad who hoards their money. Money thinks Toys' assets are obsolete and are decreasing their net worth. Toys think Money should stop working so hard and enjoy their money and finally Toys think Time is just a cheapskate who's too much of a penny pincher to enjoy the good things in life.

As you can see, my three friends don't understand that the other is simply motivated in a different way. As you read this book you'll quickly find out that I identify the most with Time, and so my Z to A plan may lean more toward my motivational style.

At this point it might be a good idea to figure out what your motivation style is. I now know that my motivator is time, but for a long time I thought it was money. I would have these great ideas and be totally motivated to them, until… I wasn't.

Here's a prime example. I have a YouTube channel called *Netnaimo*. Years ago I started making videos and at one point I was able to monetize them. It was great, the channel made me enough money to play golf all summer. Then I started focusing on the money the channel was making. All of a sudden I lost all interest in making videos. As soon as Money became the reason for making videos, it felt like work. I wasn't doing it for fun anymore. When I stopped thinking about the channel as a way to make money, the excitement came back. I don't make videos because I'm good at it, I make videos because it's a way for me to be creative and enjoy my free time.

I think this is the main reason I didn't mind going to work for someone else. A portion of the money I got from working allowed me to pay my bills, the other portion I used to invest and buy my future time. My goal was to invest as much as possible, therefore buying more time. Every time I looked at my budget I would calculate how much time I had banked so far, it was very exciting to see.

Now, I want you to really think about what *your* motivational style is. Once you know, you'll be able to build a better plan. The odds are you will not be a hundred percent of any one style, but you will lean heavier on one more than the others. It's also important to feel good about your style. If money is your motivator it doesn't mean you're greedy. If toys/things are your motivator it doesn't mean you're careless with your money and if time is your motivator it doesn't mean you're lazy. Find what motivates you and accept it.

"It's important to know what motivates _you_, not what motivates somebody else."
-Candy Crowly

"The best time to start thinking about your retirement is before the boss does."

-Anonymous

I knew I wanted to retire at some point. I wanted to enjoy the "Sweet Life". I wanted to wake up in the morning, lay in bed and revel in the pleasure of knowing that the day belonged to me. I could pretty much do whatever I wanted.

Now that I'm retired I realize that there are still many commitments in my everyday life. But that forty hours of work I used to do, equates to a lot of free time. That free time is spent doing the things I like to do like write, build crap, make videos and cook. My wife writes, sews and makes all kinds of arts and crafts stuff. We also spend a lot of time hiking and playing in the dirt.

When my wife and I retired from the "9 to 5" work world at the ages of Fifty-One and Fifty-Two, many of our friends and acquaintances wanted to know how we managed to do it. How did a couple of working stiffs manage to retire at a relatively young age? My answer was simple. Firstly we always plan for the worst and hope for the best. Secondly we try hard to live by our motto, "You can always make more money but you can't make more time." Those two statements are the bedrock of our retirement plan.

Like the majority of people out there, we've spent most of our lives selling our time to make enough money to pay for our needs. The difference with us is that we invested ninety percent of the balance into our future selves. We also worked out a plan to "work" as little as possible. What's the point of just saving for the future? We also wanted to enjoy our present lives. Personally, my goal has alway been to make enough money to supply my needs, food, lodging, travel and clothing. Once those needs are met and paid for, the rest of the time belongs to me. The biggest change came when I decided that I wanted to also meet the needs of my future self. I like that guy and I wanted him to have a good life.

I have never been the kind of worker to volunteer for overtime. As a matter of fact when I worked for Costco they would allow us to take an unpaid leave of absence in January, February and March of up to six weeks. Needless to say, but I will, I took advantage of it every year. When I returned to work after the break my co-workers asked how I managed to survive without six weeks worth of pay cheques? I explained that it didn't happen by surprise, I had a whole year to plan and save for it.

So… How, when and why did I come up with this ridiculous Z to A retirement plan idea? I'm glad I asked.

One morning I woke up and I was thirty-two. I was married with two children and had no plan to retire. In actuality, I had no long term future goals of any kind. All I knew was that I was getting older and all evidence pointed to the fact that I would keep aging as time went on. Still, sixty-five seemed like a long way away, after all I had thirty-four years to work it out and that was a long time. Then when I looked back at my life… I realized that the first thirty-one years had passed by pretty fast. The thing was that it wasn't just about me anymore. I had to plan for my wife and kids too. Hmmm… I might have to start thinking about my future. What was I going to do? Was I going to become a goal-setter?

I know a bunch of goal-setters, I mean real goal-setters. They come up with a goal, they set up a plan and they go for it. Their goal is crystal clear, they can see it, taste it, smell it, feel it, hell they can even hear it. Me? Not so much.

I mean I've tried setting goals and writing shit down and visualizing and all that stuff, but my brain just doesn't work that way. Furthermore I'm not really motivated by making money. I understand I need a certain amount to live and meet my needs, but I've never really been one of those go getters who needs to make money, money, money. To be honest, sometimes I wish I was, but I'm not.

Like I said, I tried setting goals but it just wasn't my thing. So what was I going to do? I mean I knew I didn't want to work until I died. That said, if I had to, I would. After all, I had a wife and kids to feed. I thought about it for a time and I came up with what I called my *best-worst-case-scenario*.

I thought about where I was at the present time and wondered what my sixty-five year old future self's life would look like if I didn't change anything. Work at the same job, slowly pay off my debt and rent until the day I retire. That was my best-worst-case-scenario, I now had my Z plan. It wasn't a great plan by any stretch of the imagination, but at least it was a plan.

Now that I had my Z plan, my next goal was to make an improvement on said plan. I knew enough about myself to know that any upgrade to the plan would have to be small and easy. Otherwise I'd lose focus and move on to something else and probably never think about it again. After all, I already had my retirement plan, it was to do nothing. My Z plan was… to quote Dory from Finding Nemo, "Just keep swimming." To be honest it was a pretty simple plan, I would change nothing.

I knew that my next step, the Y plan, had to improve my Z plan in some way. But how could I do something so small that it almost felt like I was doing nothing or as close to nothing as I could possibly get. The idea was to make a really small and easy change. The smaller the better this way I'd have no excuse not to do it. After just a few days I found myself moving onto plan X, then W and so on. Every letter represented an improvement and as the years went on we continued to optimize our Z plan.

As I moved down the alphabet I rewrote my best-worst-case-scenario for retirement. I figured one day if I live long enough I might reach the letter

"A" and I wondered where that would lead me. As it turns out I haven't made it there yet. I retired from my 9 to 5 job at fifty two and today we're working on our H plan. I never imagined that I'd still be improving on my Z plan one year into retirement.

I feel so blessed that I get to write this book and hopefully encourage other people to create and improve their own Z plan. As you work on your life plan remember this very important thing; we're not all built the same. We all have our own lives, our own problems, our own joys and our own dreams. It's not about being better than someone else. It's about building *your* best life. Don't let your failures or mistakes discourage you. Shit will happen and when it does you need to accept it and learn from it as soon as possible.

It's not like when I fail or something "tragic" happens in my life, I bounce back within a few seconds. I have to go through some of the stages of grief. First I deny the problem, secondly I get mad at myself for making a foolish choice. At some point I just accept that it happened and I learn from it. Sometimes it takes minutes, other times it takes days. The more often you reach the point of acceptance the quicker you'll get there the next time.

Hopefully this book will help you achieve your dream of retiring or at the very least it will give you some ideas to improve your future self's life. All you need to do is take one tiny step at a time no matter how small.

"Small daily improvements over time lead to stunning results."
-Robin Sharma

Chapter One: Nutshell

This is who I am

"Your lifetime is the only thing you truly own."

I was thirteen years old and summer vacation had just begun. My family and I lived in a low income housing strata where I spent most days playing outside. One morning I was walking around our neighborhood and happened to see a motorcycle sitting in someone's backyard. It had a flat tire, the handlebars were all rusted up and the muffler looked like Swiss cheese. I made my way through the long grass and walked over to the bike. I pulled it off the fence and sat on it. Wow, I wish this was my bike, I thought to myself.

Let me take you back one year. I was twelve years old and my sister was dating a guy who had his own motorcycle. My mom happened to be out of town visiting her sister and I was left alone with my sister. As luck would have it, her boyfriend wanted to have *private time* with her and he wanted me out of the way. He figured that if he taught me how to ride his motorcycle I would be more than happy to leave them alone. Turns out he was right.

And any time my mom wasn't around, I had a motorcycle to ride. I loved the freedom of hitting the trails with a full tank of gas. It was a great opportunity to leave everything behind. It was awesome. Every time I had to return home I found myself wishing for my own bike.

I sat on this old broken down 1972 Suzuki 185 and dreamed of being on the trails. After fifteen or twenty minutes I got off and walked away. There's no way that bike would ever be mine. About half a block away I stopped and turned back. What if the bike was just a piece of crap? What if the owner just wanted to get rid of it? Maybe I could take it away and help them with their problem.

I walked back and knocked on the door. Buddy came to the door and I asked him about the bike, he said I could have it for fifty bucks. Fifty bucks? I knew it was a great deal but it might as well have been a thousand dollars. Where was I going to get fifty bucks? My mom had five kids and could barely spare twenty-five cents.

I walked around for a while trying to figure out how to get this bike. I couldn't tell anyone about it, because I didn't want anyone knowing it was for sale. I went home and found my mom and her boyfriend sitting in the backyard enjoying the summer sun. I told my mom about the motorcycle and how I needed fifty dollars to buy it. She told me there was no way she would let me have a motorcycle let alone the fifty dollars to buy one.

After all, fifty dollars back then was like a hundred and thirty-five dollars today and when you have to feed five children… buying a "murder-cycle" for her thirteen year old son was not a place my mom was about to invest her money.

I told her how unfair it was that I couldn't have a motorcycle and after whining and complaining she said that if I could find the fifty dollars to buy the bike, she'd let me have it. Of course she knew there was no way in hell her thirteen year old son would ever be able to scrape together fifty bucks. Remember this was 1982, minimum wage was $2.00 and the unemployment rate was about 13%. My mom felt safe and secure in her decision. There was no possible way in her mind that her son would manage to save up fifty dollars, let alone fifty cents without finding something to spend it on.

I left feeling sad, but also slightly hopeful. I was halfway to owning a bike, I mean I did get permission. All I needed now was the money. I walked around most of that day trying to figure out how to get my hands on fifty dollars. I could have a yard sale and sell everything I own. That would still leave me forty nine dollars and fifty cents short. After a morning of moping I eventually found myself playing street hockey trying to forget all my foolish dreams. Later that day I made my way back home and puttered around the house. My mom's boyfriend could see that I was still working on ideas of how to make the money I needed. He called me over and offered up some advice. He suggested I get a job.

Where was I going to get a job? I didn't know anyone my age with a job. In my circle, if you wanted something, you asked your parents, if that didn't work you stole it. I woke up the next day with hopes of finding a way to own that beautiful run-down motorcycle. I went to my mom's boyfriend and I asked him for guidance. He suggested I go see the neighbor. The neighbor? Why would I ask the old guy next door for a job? The guy's yard looks like a junkyard. The only thing that place was good for was as a place to play adventure games, as long as you didn't get caught. He suggested I go knock on his door and asked him if he had any work I could do.

"Tell him you're willing to do whatever he needs." he said to me.

I was nervous about going over and never expected to get a job out of it, but at least I could tell Gerry (the boyfriend) that I tried. I knocked on the door and this old guy in his sixties answered the door. I told him I was looking for a job and that I'd do anything. He asked me why, and I told him about the motorcycle. He said he did have a job, but it was only a couple of days worth of work. He also said that I would need a letter of consent from my mom before he would let me work for him.

At first my mom said no, but Gerry convinced her that it would be safe and that a few days of work would be good for me. Since my mom couldn't read, write or speak English, Gerry wrote the note and my mom signed it. I would start working the next day.

I woke up early in the morning excited about making some money. The old man set me up with a pipe cutter and a pile of pipes. He rolled over a couple of empty oil barrels and told me to cut the pipes into four inch pieces until I filled up two barrels.

"I'll give you sixty dollars a barrel," he said. "You should be able to do one a day."

Sixty bucks a barrel? I don't think there is any way my face hid the joy and amazement of his words. To this day, I have no idea why he offered me so much money. But, true to his word, he gave me sixty dollars at the end of the first day. I ran to my buddy's place, gave him fifty bucks and dragged the bike home with me. I went back the next day and made another sixty and that's all he ever saw of me.

Not only did I have enough money to buy the bike, I had enough money to cover oil and gas for the entire summer. My sister's boyfriend helped me fix the flat tire and as for the Swiss cheese muffler, I used a few heavy gauged steel pop cans and a couple of metal hose clamps. Even back then I was building crap. (see my youtube channel: netnaimo, building crap with Chip) A couple of days later I was the proud owner of a driveable motorcycle.

Even back then I was a *time* motivated person. I have spent all of my life trying to figure out how to work just enough to have my needs met. Free time was and still is the most important thing to me. It's not that I don't work hard, I just want to work "hard" as little as possible. As it turns out this whole book is about how I worked to buy my future self free time.

When I moved out at eighteen, I got a job that gave me just enough hours to cover my rent, insurance on my motorcycle, a bit of food and of course a case of beer and pack of smokes every weekend.

Sadly I didn't always know my boundaries and at one point I ended up homeless for about six months or so... but that's another story for another time.

Looking back on my life I can clearly see that autonomy of time has always had a priority over money. I just didn't become fully conscious of that fact until I was in my forties.

Many people have asked me; if time is my motivator, why do I talk about money all the time? My answer is that I need money to buy my future self time. I do this by investing and creating as many passive income streams as I can. Ergo, free time is my true motivator.

"It's really clear that the most precious resource we all have is time.

-Steve jobs

Chapter Two: Brainwaves

It's just how my brain works

"Nobody is superior, nobody is inferior, but nobody is equal either. People are simply unique, incomparable. You are you, I am me."-
Osho

Have you ever done a puzzle maze? I have always found it easier to find my way out by starting from the finish line and making my way to the start. Some say that doing so is cheating because the puzzle was built to be started at the start and finished at the finish line. I never accepted that.

Whenever I was given a puzzle, I would set my pencil down at the start and try... then after a couple of attempts I'd head to the finish line and work my way backwards to the start Point in no time flat.

Who knew my retirement plan would work out the same way?

"We are all different... That is what makes us the same."
-Anonymous

Chapter Three: Plan Z

May 2001- In the beginning

"If you don't know where you are going, you will probably end up somewhere else." – Lawrence J. Peter

When I was twenty five I believed that I would be financially independent by the time I was thirty. I had one basic goal; find an idea that would make me an easy Million and… make it quick please.

For some unknown reason I believed a Million dollars would solve all my problems. So, my plan was to make a Million, quit my job and then sit back and enjoy the rest of my life. By the time I was in my late twenties, I started to appreciate how hard it was to make a "quick" million. As every year passed that million dollar dream seemed to be less and less realistic. I was so sure that my next idea would be the one.

What kind of things did I try? You'll be glad I asked. Let's see… we were website designers, graphic designers, we had an online store. I had ideas like the "QCR" Quick Card Resume, it was a resume on a business card. That brainchild made me about $500.00, not quite the million I was going for. We made menus, murals, chalk art, I invested in penny stocks, created "wildcrib" a cribbage game. We also produced pamphlets, comic books, puzzles, magazines, advertising, reusable window art and the list goes on and on.

My problem has never been coming up with ideas, I have plenty of those. My problem is following through with my ideas. I would spend a few months working on something and then a shiny object would distract me. Suddenly I'd be working on some new idea. Of course my latest creation was always my best idea ever.

I couldn't figure myself out. When I worked for others, I gave it my all, but when it came to working for myself... I tend to chill out a lot more and when you're trying to make a million dollars, chilling out is not the quickest way to reach your goal. I was always onto the next big idea, even before the ink dried on the present idea I was working on. Years later (in my forties again) I realized my problem. I was chasing the money. I thought that money was my driver. But as soon as money became the focus and not the joy of creating, I would lose interest. It wasn't fun anymore and so I would move on to something worth spending my time doing.

From the time I got married at twenty five, to the time we started our Z plan a lot of stuff happened in our lives. To keep it short, I'll give you a quick rundown.

1. I got married
2. Came up with a plethora of million dollar ideas
3. We had a child
4. We quit our jobs to start our art/website design business that would generate millions of dollars
5. We ran out of money
6. I became depressed
7. We ended up on welfare
8. Our daughter was diagnosed with a brain tumor
9. She passed away
10. The depression got worse
11. We drank heavily and racked up almost thirty thousand dollars in credit card debt
12. And on and on…

When my wife was pregnant with our second child, I started to realize that I had to figure out a way to live again. I needed to find a way of coping with the sadness and depression of losing a child. I had to get back into the world. I had to find a job and support my family, I had to move forward.

Right after our daughter was born I got a job at a jewelry store over the Christmas season. I knew right away this was not going to last. I had way too much energy to stand behind a counter, selling something I didn't believe in. I ended up quitting that job and finding one as a driver for The Sally Ann. I picked up food for the soup kitchen in the morning and worked at the thrift store in the afternoon. I didn't care that it was a minimum wage job. I just needed to work somewhere and figure myself out. I thought I'd only be there a few months. As it turned out, a few months turned into two years. We now had our third child coming and I was still kinda lost. I was thirty-two years old with no clue where my life was going.

That's when my wife and I sat down and started talking about where our lives were going and how we needed to make plans for our family's future and our eventual retirement. As a couple and family we were pretty happy. Financially, we were slowly sinking deeper and deeper into debt.

I had no idea how to make plans for the future. I tried for years to make that magical million, but the only thing I accomplished was digging myself into a deep financial hole.

Like many people do, I turned to books for help. I read all kinds of savings, investing and retirement books. Years before I had read Think and Grow Rich and all the other books that were just rewrites of that great Napoleon Hill classic. Somehow, it just didn't work for me. It motivated me for a short period of time, but that's just not how my brain works. I couldn't visualize myself Into anything. I am not a visual thinker, I am a verbal thinker. My wife can close her eyes and see images in finite detail, when I close my eyes I see the back of my eyelids.

I had to find a way to solve this seemingly unsolvable puzzle that was my future. I had to engineer a way for me to set a goal and achieve it. But how? Then it hit me… What if I start from the end and work my way backwards? What if I just drew out my best-worst-case-scenario? What if I started by not changing anything? What if I started my life maze at the end and worked my way to today?

At first my wife was a little confused, but she went along. After all, a plan no matter how bad it is, is still better than no plan. At least we would have a starting point.

In September of 2001, we sat down and created our best-worst-case-scenario or "Retirement Plan Z". At this point in my life I was thirty-two, my wife was a thirty one year old stay at home mom and we had two kids, one age two and the other one month old.

This is what our Z plan looked like at the time.

- I work for minimum wage until I'm 65.
- We rent our whole lives *(An apartment in a building not a house). This way we can minimize the risk of people selling the building and having to move. This will also keep the rent reasonable.*
- Raise the kids and see them move out on their own.

- Slowly and methodically pay off all our debts.
  (*At the time we had just over $25,000.00 of credit card debt at 20% interest rate. At the rate we were going it would have taken us 21 years to pay off the debt and we would have paid about $81,000.00 in interest.*)
- We'd be debt free when I was fifty-three years old.
- We'd start saving for retirement then. (*Our plan was to invest the money we'd been using to pay off our credit card debt.*) That would give us twelve years to save for retirement. We could save around $50,000.00 or more.
- Over the course of 33 years, we'd use our spare time to work on writing, creating videos, doing art and other things we enjoy. At sixty-five we'd do more of it.

We did it, plan Z, it wasn't complicated. Already we could see that it would be very possible to save $50,000.00 for our retirement. That alone was something to be excited about.

With plan Z in hand we were able to relax for a day or two and let the new plan sink in. I told a few friends about it and they chuckled at my idea. The basic responses were:

"That's your plan?"

My reply was, "What's your retirement plan?" Turns out they didn't "need" one.

The other popular comment was, "Can you set the bar any lower?"

"Where is your bar set?" Turns out they didn't have one.

The comments from the peanut gallery didn't really bother me. I had a plan and that was good enough for me.

Before I end this chapter I have to say that there is one consistent thing I've noticed in the last thirty odd years… and let me tell you there have been a few odd ones.

People who blame others for their misfortunes tend to be the ones who discourage you from moving on and up. The successful people I've met in my life have always encouraged me to dream and go for it, no matter how big or small that dream was.

"A goal is not always meant to be reached; it often serves simply as something to aim at."

—Bruce Lee

Chapter Four:
Another Dimension

Try to see things from a different perspective

"No problem can be solved from the same level of consciousness that created it." -Albert Einstein

I chatted with my daughter one day and wanted to know if she was a natural born pessimist or an optimist. So, I showed her a glass half filled with water and I asked her if the glass was half full or half empty.

She looked at the glass then at me. She went back and forth a few times and I could see a look of confusion on her face. After a few moments I asked her, "Well, is it half full or half empty?"

She said, "It all depends on your goal. If your goal is to drink it all up, then I would say it's half empty. If your goal is to fill it, I would say it's half full."

I thought about it for a moment then I said, "Go to your room smart ass."

"Your perspective will either become your prison or your passport."
-Steven Furtick

Chapter Five: Plan Y

How I made $53,000.00 in less than three hours! Kinda.

"Here is an equation worth remembering:
Five dollars earned minus seven dollars spent
equals an unhappy life."
- Jon Morrison

Plan Z was simply to change nothing, live life as I was and retire at 65. If I wanted a better outcome all I had to do was change something. Anything. As long as that *something* didn't take up too much of my time. I knew that if I wanted to improve on my Z plan, I'd have to trick myself into doing it.

But how? I was too ADHD to set big lofty financial goals. I knew from past experience that any goal that made money the focus and took *time away* from my *free time* would end up a goal-unrealized. I needed a change that was relatively quick to do, was small and simple… just like me. If I was going to reach a point in my life where I could call it a day and start enjoying my post-work years, it would have to be done on my terms.

I am a verbal thinker. When someone asks what my next move is or what I'm planning to do over the next year I start to throw out all my ideas at once. As I babble on, people tend to shake their heads in dismay, they stop making eye contact and slowly back away.

"You can't do everything." or "What do you really want?" are things I hear all the time.

"It's a fireworks of ideas." I say as I look up and watch my shimmering, twinkling fingers. Then I haphazardly pick some sparkles from the sky. I raise my eyebrows in joy, "So many choices."

I guess what I'm trying to say is, focusing on something for a long time is not my strong point. It just wasn't in me to come up with the ultimate dream plan and focus on it until I got there. I mean, don't get me wrong, I wanted to retire as early as possible. The question was how do I do it in a way that works for me.

I love learning, I love reading books and asking people I meet tons of questions about their lives. I also tend to hyperfocus, for example one year I only read books about the brain. Books like: My stroke of insight by Jill Bolte Taylor Ph.D, The brain's way of healing and The brain that changes itself by Norman Doidge, M.D., books on autism, social development and the list goes on. It seems every year I hyperfocus on a different subject.

You think I could hyperfocus on a retirement "Plan A"… but alas it's not so. Or is it? As it turns out, in a strange way, all my goals from Z down were really "A" goals of sorts. I mean if you think about it, if I had stopped at Z and ended my life there, in a way, that would have been my A goal. But I digress. Did I mention I'm ADHD?

How was I going to improve my Z plan? I had to make the upgrade small and easy. It couldn't be too time consuming or life changing. I didn't want my retirement planning interfering with my life. The concept was not how to create a *full-color* A plan. It was about creating a multitude of small improvements to the Z plan. The dream was simply to retire as early as possible. If that was retiring at sixty-five, then so be it.

Again I want to remind you that everyone is different. Don't compare your ideas of retirement with others. Many people have said to us, "Oh, I wish I was you."

Our response is usually, if you wanted to be us, you'd be living like us. But you're not us, you are you. Live like you. Plan *you* from Z to A.

I have a few millionaire friends who seem to work eighteen hour days, seven days a week. Some are CEOs, others are investors, land developers etc. They all claim to love what they do and they tell me it's not work, it's pure pleasure.

I watch them run around and do what they do and to be honest it looks a lot like work. I don't want their lifestyle and they don't want mine. That's why I will continue to remind you that we all have our own ideas of what a nice life is. Don't try to be someone else. Don't worry about what others want. Think about what you want and what makes you happy.

Ok, back to the story. How would my Y plan improve on my Z plan? After a week or so, it hit me, **debt**! What if I reduced my debt load? I figured the quicker I did that, the less I'd be paying in interest charges. But how? I wasn't going to take on another job. I was working a forty hour work week and that was more than enough thank-you. I wasn't ready to start looking for a higher paying job either. I was comfortable and I got my pick of holiday time. So how could I reduce my debt with the money I was already making? Increasing the payment wasn't really an option; we were barely making ends meet. Some months they didn't meet at all.

As I saw it at the time I had two choices. The first was debt consolidation. I really didn't want to do that. I didn't feel comfortable having to commit to mandatory payments over many years. I really wanted to stay in control of my own finances. Getting a line of credit was not an option, I had way too much debt vs income. The second solution I came up with was paying less interest. It was an idea, but how does one go about paying less interest?

The rest of the day I toyed with the idea of calling the credit card companies and asking for a reduction in my interest rate. When I got home I told my wife about the idea and she encouraged me to go ahead and try. I did a little research on the internet and realized it was possible to negotiate a better deal with the credit card companies.

Plan Y would be calling all three credit card companies. I was ready to go all in and commit three hours of my day to making phone calls. As the moment of truth got close I could feel myself getting anxious. I decided to write down my negotiating points, I figured that would keep me from being too distracted and rambling on. My main arguments were One: I was finding it hard to make the payments. Two: I was looking into having my debt consolidated. Three: It would be in their best interest to cut my interest rate a little. If I did get my debt consolidated they would lose money in the long run.

I took a few deep breaths and psyched myself up and made the calls. As it turns out I was able to get my interest rates reduced on two out of three cards. Instead of paying an average rate of 20% interest, I was now averaging 14%.

That's the only thing I did that week. After all I had to muster up the courage to make the call and that took a lot out of me. Don't forget I had to put in almost three hours of work. Mind you most of that time was spent on hold.

I Felt like a real winner. I was so excited. I had executed my first big deal. Plan Y was to make three phone calls. Mission accomplished.

We sat down and upgraded our Z plan. One small step, one giant impact. Instead of paying over $81,000.00 in interest over twenty-two years, I would now be paying about $43,000.00 in interest in eighteen years. Not only did I save money, I also saved time. I could be debt free four years sooner. This would add time for my retirement savings.

Plan Y had a domino effect that I hadn't really thought through before I made the calls.

1. I was saving around $38,000.00 in interest payments.
2. I saved four years of payments.
3. I added an extra four years of saving time for my retirement. That could add up to $15,000.00 more to our retirement pot.

I could hardly believe it. It felt like I had just made $53,000.00 in less than three hours. Sure it was $53,000.000 spread out over thirty-three years, nevertheless that still averaged out to almost $1,600.00 a year in savings. I was happy to have it or at least happy not to pay it out.

I'll probably say this more times than you care to hear it… but here goes. Everyone is different and we all want different things. Everybody has their own ideas of what the perfect retirement life is going to be. I know some folks who never want to retire. They want to work until they die. (I don't understand them.) But I don't have too. The question is always, what is <u>your</u> retirement going to look like?

Let your Z plan be your guide. Work on improving it over the next few years. Don't be surprised if you change your mind as you move forward. Your ideas about retirement will probably need to change depending on how much time you have, change with it.

When we first started our Z plan, we never imagined retiring at fifty-two and fifty-three. By no means did we think we'd ever leave BC and move to Ontario. I guess what I'm trying to say is, "Enjoy the ride your plans take you on."

"If you think nobody cares if you're alive, try missing a couple of car payments." - Earl Wilson

Chapter Six: Aim at something

A plan is better than no plan.

"Good fortune is what happens when opportunity meets with planning."
-Thomas Edison

With the Y plan accomplished and the Z plan readjusted, I sat back and thought about how one little change made such a huge difference in my life. It gave a boost of confidence that made me think I could possibly be on to something. Goal-setting might not be as complicated as I once thought it was. If only I'd known before.

I had come a long way from those crazy days of my youth. There was a time back in my late teens and early twenties when I worked as a dishwasher. I was lucky enough to have a roommate to help pay the bills for a while. My problem was that I thought drugs, alcohol and partying were more important than rent and food. My wants overpowered my needs. Living this way for just a few months got me to where I was unemployed, my roommate moved out and soon enough I was secretly living out of my dad's garage.

I would sneak in at night and creep out early in the morning. I'd walk the streets, hit up some friends with the hope of finding some mind altering drug that would take me away from my situation, for any amount of time. If I couldn't find a couch to sleep on I'd head out and somehow I'd find my way back to the garage. Not my best moments. For the next few years I bounced from job to job, city to city, room to room and couch to couch, until I was twenty-two.

One day, something clicked. I was out searchin' for my daily dose of mind-altering-something-or-other and I had a very strong and discouraging thought. I might have to spend the day sober. That's when I realized that this wasn't the life I wanted for myself. I knew there was someone better inside of me. I *needed* to find that person. It wasn't easy, but as you can see... I made it out alive.

So why am I telling you all this? I want you to know that wherever you are right now in life, you too can change into the person you really want to be. You have an opportunity to set yourself up for a better day and a better future. Start by making <u>one</u> change to improve your life plan.

I don't know where you are in life. I don't know how old you are, where you come from or what you've been through or what you are going through. I do believe that if you make your Z plan and work on making small changes you can make a difference in your own life. Regardless of how many small changes you make, you'll have a better life than having done nothing at all.

I'm not going to say that you're going to make it and that everything will be great in the end. I will say that it will be better. I am not going to say that if you put it out in the universe it's going to come true because the universe has no choice but to give you what you want if you just ask for it. I will say that if you work and change and move forward and put it out there and talk about it and ask for help, people will help and things will happen. I won't say, "Everything happens for a reason." I will say, "You can give reason to everything that happens."

I do believe that if you share your plans with everyone you know, good things will come about. If you make an effort to talk to strangers, you'll be introduced to new possibilities. If you ask people to help you with your vision, people will help. If you take even the tiniest step forward, your situation will improve. Change will come. I can't tell you the exact moment in time when it will happen, but it will happen. The trick is to keep moving forward. Start slow and allow yourself to gain momentum. Does that mean that you won't falter? No. Everybody fails and falls. Without failure, there is no success. Most importantly there is no shame in failure.

"It takes as much energy to wish
as it does to plan."
-Eleanor Roosevelt

Chapter Seven: Plan X

January 2002 - Plan X What else could I do?

"Money cannot buy peace of mind. It cannot heal ruptured relationships or build meaning into a life that has none." - Richard DeVos

The anxiety of making the dreaded phone calls of Plan Y were now behind us. In hindsight it really wasn't that hard to do, although it didn't feel that way at the time. With our future selves in mind, we decided to continue to focus our attention on creating plan X.

I thought about it for a week or so. I had a hard time coming up with any ideas. I mean what else could I do that was as easy or easier than making a few phone calls?

After a while my thoughts came back to our credit card debt. Was there something else I could do to reduce the amount of interest I was paying or was there a way I could pay off my credit cards faster?

As I pointed out earlier, I wasn't prepared to take on another job and I couldn't increase my payments any more. There were some months we couldn't make the minimum payment. I had figured out a work-around for those times. Here's what I did; we used to make a payment on the card using our grocery and other bills money and then use the card to buy groceries and pay bills. At least it looked like we were making the minimum payment. Before our interest rates went down, we were putting about $450.00 a month on the cards, with about $400.00 of that going to interest.

Now that our interest was averaging 14% we only paid about $300 in interest a month. I realized that in a year or so I could reduce my payments a little and put more money in my pocket. But then I thought, what if I don't reduce my payment? What if I just continue to make the $450.00 a month payment until the cards are all paid up?

That's when plan X was born. As soon as I got home I got out my calculator and did some quick math. If I paid $450.00 a month, I could pay off my debt in eight years. I'd pay out about $16,000.00 in interest. That was a whopping $27,000.00 in savings on top of what I'd save with plan Y. I could be debt free by the time I was 40. Was it possible? I would have twenty five years to save up for my retirement. I could possibly save up to $135,000.00 by my sixty-fifth birthday.

Plan X was actually less work than plan Y. How was it possible that doing nothing (or at least not changing anything) could possibly net me such a huge windfall? Of course plan X was also about not putting any more money on the cards. We'd have to find a way to live within our means.

I would love for you to move on to the next chapter believing that eight years later I was debt free and on my way to saving for retirement. Alas, 'twas not so. As it turns out, life got in the way a few times and being debt free was not as easy as I had hoped and planned it out to be.

Our lives included a few humps, bumps and potholes along the way. There were months that were a little tougher than others and there were times where we just wanted to forget about how poor we were and just spend a few bucks and live life to its fullest. However we also knew that doing so would destroy our dreams of a better life. So, every time we fell off the horse, we'd dust ourselves off and get back on the debt reduction horse again. Although plan X was the third step in our retirement improvement idea, it went on for years.

Every time we fell, we got up and as it happens, the more you fall the quicker you learn to get up. We were constantly reminding ourselves that (Failure x Repetition = Success).

After about eight months of working on it I knew I had to create another plan to keep us moving forward. As it turns out, my wife created plan W and it was a Whopper!

"Everytime you borrow money, you're robbing your future self." -Nathan Morris

Chapter Eight: Unacceptable

Why is it taboo to talk about money?

"For the love of money is the root of all kinds of evil." -1 Timothy 6:10

Why is it that we don't like talking about money? Is it that some of us make so little of it that we're embarrassed to talk about it? Could it be that we're deep in debt, and are ashamed that we can't make ends meet? Is it that we may be getting by and we have no idea how we're doing it? Maybe we're on the verge of bankruptcy and don't want to admit it to others, let alone ourselves. Of course there are a few people that make tons of money and they just don't want to rub it in our faces.

I find it interesting that most people don't want to talk about how much money they have. They'll avoid eye contact when I mention debt. Most people won't share their hourly wage or salary information. Interestingly enough though, they sure are happy to tell me about their latest deal and how much they "saved" on their new "thing". They'll spend hours telling me about how they're always getting value for their money. We have all witnessed over and over how people are so dismissive about their personal finances, but are eager to help "save us into poverty." I only wish they were as enthusiastic about helping me put away funds for a healthier retirement.

If we want to do better with money we need to talk. We need to end this taboo that says it's impolite to talk about money. According to Fidelity Investments, 43 percent of Americans don't know how much money their spouse makes, yet the number three reason people get divorced is money issues.

If you don't know where your money is going... someone will find a way to make it go into their pockets. We shouldn't be shy about the money we make or the debt we have. No one knows everything about money. So, the more we talk about it the more ideas we get, the more tools we have the more money wise we become.

Money is a tool and like any other tool, when we know how to use it properly we can build better things. In our family we use money in the following ways, of course there are always exceptions to every rule. First, it's a way to purchase the things we need: rent, food, hydro, etc. Second, build wealth. Third, helping others. Fourth, buying wants.

People tend to spend their money and never really think about it. Do you know how much you spent on groceries last month? How much money went into your gas tank? Can you tell me how much you spent on booze or restaurants? No? Well you'll be happy to hear that you're in the majority. Turns out 51% of the Canadian population has no idea either.

I'll give you one more statistic before we move on. The average Canadian household debt represented 177 percent of disposable income in 2019. Household debt increased to 180 percent of gross income in 2022.

What does that mean? It means that for every $1,000.00 you made (gross/before taxes come off) in 2022, you probably owed $1,800.00.

Think about it. First you pay your taxes, then you get your take-home pay. At that point you pay interest on your mortgage, credit cards, line of credit, car, etc. Once that's done, you pay the principal of your mortgage, credit card... you get the idea. After all that, you pay for food, cable, phone, blah, blah, blah, blah. It's enough to make your head spin. Yet, we don't talk about it or seek help.

So many of us are using money like a hammer, when it should be used as a saw.

"Don't go broke trying to look rich."

-Anonymous

Chapter Nine: Plan W

Sept 2002, Buy a what?

"The best time to buy a house is always five years ago." -Ray Brown

We were about nine months into plan X when my wife mentioned the idea of buying a house. I was like, "Plan Y was three phone calls and plan X was changing nothing. See where I'm going?" I was kinda hoping that plan W was going to be me doing less than nothing. I had a feeling it wasn't going to be that easy.

My wife wanted to upgrade our plan Z from *renting for life* to *owning a home*. It didn't take me long to point out that we didn't have any real savings, let alone money for a down payment. We were struggling to make ends meet. How the heck were we going to buy a house? She was quick to remind me how much I loved to solve problems. I in turn reminded her that I was not a miracle worker.

I didn't want to dismiss her idea of home ownership, after all this was a team effort and I had to show support for her ideas. I really do like coming up with out of the box ideas to solve problems, but this one seemed out of reach for me.

I spent the next few days analyzing the situation and looking at it from multiple angles. I thought about it all day long every day. Every idea I came up with seemed enormous, time consuming and mostly unrealistic.

It was very important (for me anyhow) that every step be easy and small. Days turned into weeks. I felt anxious about the idea. It was just too big a step. Maybe this whole Z to A plan was nothing more than another one of my crazy ideas that had run its course.

One day I told her that there was no way we could buy a house in the near future. We would have to come up with some other idea for plan W. She refused. She wasn't going to give up so easily. She encouraged me and reminded me that we could do almost anything if we put our minds on it.

We talked about our fears, possible setbacks and all the obstacles in our way. Once we started expressing our worries out loud we were able to see them for what they were, solvable problems. We reminded each other again and again that Failure x Trying = Success. I do need to say something about $F \times T = S$. This doesn't mean that you will necessarily be successful at achieving your goal; to me it means more that $F \times S$ is in itself Success. It means not giving up on moving forward.

By the end of the night we'd come to the conclusion that even if we never got a house we would still come out ahead because we'd be focusing on debt reduction and saving for a down payment.

I slept much better that night. The next day I got back to thinking about ways of getting that house. I wasn't going to give up. At the time I was making minimum wage and we were thousands of dollars in debt. How could we put ourselves in a position to buy a house?

After a few more days of thinking the stress started to build again. Then I thought wait a minute. I'm only a few months into this Z to A planning and I'm already working on plan W… how cool is that? I was thinking about this whole thing the wrong way. Buying a house was not *one* giant event. It wasn't *one* thing, it was dozens, maybe even hundreds of small steps. Everything we do in life is all just a bunch of small events that lead to something big.

Over the next few days I daydreamed about sitting in our very own place. I did my best to imagine the feeling of home ownership. Being a verbal thinker I talked about it with friends and coworkers. I knew it was important to think, talk and dream of what I wanted. There is no way to reach a goal unless you think about it and move towards it.

What if we could find a cheaper place to live? This would allow us to put more money into debt reduction and I could increase my RRSP deductions at work. The RRSP portion would work as a tax deduction and we might be able to use that money for a down payment. I was determined that the biggest and hardest part of this whole idea would actually be the physical move itself.

Over the next few months we talked to everyone we knew about our need for cheaper accommodations. Word got around and a few weeks later a friend introduced us to a woman who was looking at moving back east for two years. She was in need of a house sitter. We were in a situation where we could be saving two hundred and fifty dollars a month, freeing up six thousand dollars over two years.

At first we thought that having to move in two years was a bit of a pain, but then we realized that this could actually work in our favor. Having a time limit gave us a checkered flag, a finish line. It was possible that a sense of urgency could push us to achieve this goal.

Two years wasn't a lot of time to get ourselves out of debt and build up tons of savings. However, it was an opportunity for us to improve our situation. We decided to move. We also set a goal for home ownership within two years. We knew our goal was idealistic. We reasoned that in two years we'd either move into a new rental or a new house. In any case we'd have to move again.

Looking back it seemed like finding a cheaper place and moving was such a large step. Yet the fact of the matter is that I wasn't doing anything dramatic. There was no big "aha" moment, it was all just tiny steps here and there. The reality was all we did was talk to everyone we met and let them know what we needed. As it turns out, our need was an answer to someone else's need. You gotta love a win/win situation.

Our greatest tool has always been supporting each other's ideas, even when they seem a little outlandish.

By the spring of 2003 we were official house sitters. We did our best to invest our extra savings into debt reduction and RRSPs. That same year we became proud parents of our first kindergartener. Regrettably school came with a cost, like outings, pizza days etc. To help pay for the school stuff, Sharla sold portraits, and took our youngest out in her stroller to go bottle picking almost everyday. We were determined to make it happen.

Although plan W wasn't putting us into our own home straight away, it put us on the right path. We felt that the two years of house sitting would improve our Z plan no matter what the final outcome was. It was now time to move on to plan V.

"You must gain control over your money or the lack of it will forever control you."

-Dave Ramsey

Chapter Ten: IOU

There is good debt and bad debt... Spoiler alert: Most of it is bad

"Debt is the worst poverty." -Thomas Fuller

Buying a house to live in is usually a good investment. But there are times when this is not so. Buying a house that's valued at $100,000.00 and paying $200,000.00, just because the realtor says things like: "That's the market right now.", "Bid higher so you don't lose it.", "Don't worry, house prices will never go down.", "You've been approved for $X , use it all up." and other crap like that is not a reason to buy. Remember realtors work on commission. So basically they are used car salespeople, except with a much bigger commission.

Their number one tactic is feeding off your F.O.M.O. (Fear Of Missing Out). They are utilizing a well known marketing trigger. It's called playing with your emotions. It's a well known fact that most of us make purchases big and small based on emotion. I know what you're thinking. There is no way *you* would ever buy something as big as a house based on emotions. *You* wouldn't fall for that, you'd make *your* decision based solely on logic. The truth is you'd be wrong.

As sad as it is to say, we are creatures of habit. According to Harvard professor Gerald Zaltman, 95% of purchasing decisions are made based on emotions. If you think about it for a minute, I'm sure you'll agree that it's a very dangerous way to buy 95% of the stuff we buy. Especially when that thing could be worth thousands of dollars.

According to a citnow.com blog on car selling:

"Buying a car tends to be considered as more of a rational purchase, which means it's the head that rules the heart. The customer wants to secure the best deal possible, in what is normally a significant financial commitment. But emotional factors have a much bigger influence than many people think – or perhaps, more than they'd like to admit."

Remember the housing bubble of 2008? No? Here's a very oversimplified way of explaining some of the housing issues that happened then. People bought houses with little or no money down. The banks lent money to pretty much anyone who asked. "Don't worry man... you can never lose buying a house and interest rates are low." and "In a couple of years you'll be able to pull out tons of equity or resell it for way more. You'll make a killing."

So, people bought houses. Then, the shit hit the fan. Thousands upon thousands lost their jobs during the great recession. Because of the low interest rates people had been racking up debt. Their plan was to pull out all their home equity to pay off the debt in the future. The only problem was they had no equity. In fact many homes lost value. As if from out of nowhere millions of people filed for foreclosure. According to CNN Money, 1 out of every 54 homes was lost. People literally abandoned their houses and handed the keys over to the banks. Things got so bad that in 2013 the city of Detroit entered bankruptcy after a state-appointed emergency manager displaced local elected officials from power and chose not to pay $300,000,000.00 due on the city's debt. So, ya it was a big deal.

Isn't it crazy that people will spend more time picking a movie to watch on Netflix, than they will thinking through the long term consequences of buying a house? (*Ok, I'm exaggerating a little, but you get the picture.*)

The next time you have to pay out a large sum of money for something you want to buy, try to imagine yourself ten years into the future. Think about the costs associated with the decisions you are making today. What happens if you lose your job, will you still be able to pay your debt? How will the choices of today affect you five, ten, fifteen years down the road? The odds are that if you do think hard about it, you'll make a better decision. Trust me your future self will be grateful.

2008 in a hundred words or less...

The housing crash was caused by a variety of things, including predatory lending practices targeting low-income homebuyers, excessive risk-taking by the financial institution and the bursting of the US housing bubble.

Mortgage-backed securities tied to American real estate, as well as derivatives linked to those securities, collapsed in value.

Things were a little different in canada.

"Your future depends on what you do today."

-Mahatma Gandhi

Chapter Eleven: Plan V

Sept 2003 - Buying a house is not easy.

"The pessimist sees difficulty in every opportunity.
The optimist sees opportunity in every difficulty." -Winston Churchill

A year had passed by so quickly. My wife and I were getting pretty excited about the thought of buying a house, but reality soon sunk in. I was bringing in about $1,200.00 a month and since our income was low, the Canadian government gave us a monthly child tax credit of $500.00. Therefore I was bringing in just over twenty thousand a year. Even if our credit cards would have had a zero interest rate, we couldn't have paid them off in a year even if we put a hundred percent of our income on them. Damn you reality checks!

Never having bought a house we needed to become more educated on the ins and outs. We took it upon ourselves to meet with a mortgage broker and he told us exactly what we knew. He looked over our finances and tax returns and after he stopped laughing, he told us there was no way we could get a mortgage for at *least* two more years. He explained that lenders wanted to see consistency in your work environment. In other words, I had to be at my job for at least five years before they would even talk to us (especially at our level of income). He suggested Sharla get a job. However for us that was out of the question. We had agreed before having children that one of us would stay home at least until both kids were in school. Our number one priority was to be there for the kids. I told him I was thinking of looking for a better paying job, but he said I should suck it up for two more years otherwise I'd have to start all over at zero.

When we got home that afternoon we were a little down. We didn't think it was possible to reduce our debt enough to please the banks *and* save for a downpayment. As she often did, my wife reminded me again that I loved problem solving. Alright… I told her to give me a few days to think about it. Over the next few days we bounced all kinds of ideas off of each other. One day I came home and announced that I'd found a solution. We'd contact Habitat for Humanity.

Over the next couple of weeks Sharla did some research, made some calls and sent out a few emails. Soon we had an interview. I must say that it was somewhat humbling to make the call, but we were thinking of our family and our future.

By the way… (spoiler alert), it turns out, we were too poor for Habitat for Humanity. Yes, you read that right. Talk about a kick in the nuts. Let me tell you… if I thought making the call was humbling? Try sitting through a person telling you that your finances are in such bad shape that even an organization that helps poor people can't help you. *Ouch!*

Of course the woman interviewing us was very polite and gentle with us. She pointed out all the reasons why they couldn't help us out. As she was leaving she told us to try again in a couple of years, maybe things would be different. I told her not to worry, they wouldn't be hearing from us again. I told her that we'd have a house within the next year. She just smiled and said, "Good luck with that."

When I closed the door I turned to my wife and said something like, "That's fucking bullshit." I quickly realized I wasn't mad at Habitat, I was mad at me. After all, the poor woman didn't do anything wrong. It would have been much easier to stay mad at her and blame Habitat for Humanity for my failings, but at some point I'd have to accept responsibility for my own actions.

Plan V was turning out to be a little more difficult than just making a call or two. Or was it? A couple of months went by and I was still struggling to find a solution to our housing problem. We had until the summer of 2005 to make it happen and time was ticking away pretty fast. Then one day my buddy Tom, whom I worked with said, "Why don't you ask your parents or in-laws to co-sign for you?"

That's crazy, I thought. But during the next couple of days my wife and I talked about it and we decided to call my step-father. He had money and would surely co-sign. I made the call and (after he stopped laughing) he said no. Of course I couldn't really blame him. He pretty much knew me as a guy who couldn't hold down a job, drank a lot, did drugs and was homeless for a while. He knew I'd changed over the years, but when you live five thousand kilometers apart and never see each other… Past memories are all you really have and it's hard to change your paradigm about someone you don't interact with often. Oh well.

Our second choice was asking Sharla's parents. We invited them over. We sat down and talked to them about co-signing. We opened up our books and showed them how we were paying down our debt, putting some money into RRSPs and showed them three years worth of bills and rent. They could clearly see that we'd never missed a payment. We explained that our goal of owning a house could actually reduce our cost of living. We wanted to find a place that was cheaper than the present rent we were paying. We told them that if they did co-sign we would set a goal to get them off the mortgage within five years. They agreed to be our co-signers.

Within a month we were sitting down with a mortgage broker trying to figure out how much we could borrow. I have to mention that at the time (for a very short window) the Canadian government allowed the banks to "lend" the buyer the down payment for a house. The downpayment was added to the cost of the mortgage.

The broker told us that we qualified for a mortgage of up to two hundred and fifty thousand dollars. We knew that was way more than we could safely afford. We didn't want to spend more than a hundred and twenty-five thousand dollars. We wanted to find a place that we could truly afford, one that could be paid on one income at minimum wage.

The search was on. We looked at rundown shacks, mobile homes and even trailers. Then one day while doing research I found this old side by side. It was on a cul-de-sac, had a huge back yard and was priced like it was a former crack house. It turns out it was a *present* crack house.

I will not go into the details of how messy, dirty, stinky and disgusting the place was or how we had our own pet cemetery in the crawlspace. I'll barely mention the urine soaked floors and… well I'm sure you get the idea.

Sharla made an appointment to see the place while I was at work. She was in love. The realtor thought she was crazy. That night, we both went back to look at it with the realtor. Another couple showed up before us, we waited in the car and watched as their realtor opened the door. They immediately turned around and were gagging from the stench. Needless to say, they walked away without making an offer. "I think that's a good sign for us." I said, smiling at my wife.

In Aug of 2005 we were moving into our own place. (BTW our attached neighbor Judy and her daughter became part of our family. We lived in peace for the entire sixteen years we were there.)

The first thing we did was pull the carpets out of the kids' room. We needed them to have a clean, safe place where they could sleep and play while we worked on the house. What a mess… the closet had been used as a kitty litter box. No box, just kitty litter spread across the closet floor. Lucky for us our friends had dealt with cat urine in the place they bought and still had some neutralizer left over (for free). The in-laws were a big help. They bought us paint and even helped us clean up the place. Badda-bing, badda-boom, the girls had a place to play and sleep.

Over the next few months my wife worked all day every day cleaning and painting and pulling and fixing. At one point there were no more carpets, no more dead cats in the crawl space and the 5,500 square foot backyard with the five foot grass and blackberry vines was mostly cleaned up.

Although we dreamed about home ownership, we never truly believed it would happen in the span of the two years. It did strengthen our belief that as long as we tried and moved forward, almost anything was possible.

Before I close up this chapter I know some of you might be thinking things like:

- They got lucky, they had in-laws to co-sign.
- The government allowed them to buy without a real down payment.
- They got a cheap place to rent.
- Things were less expensive back then.
- Etc…

But remember YOUR plan, YOUR tiny steps. The best way to find gold is to look for it. Every story will be different. Set your goals and go for it. You never know what's waiting for you out there.

"Poverty is not a hindrance to success"

-Filipino Proverb.

Chapter Twelve: Target Practice

Am I a goal setter?

"You don't have to see it to believe it"

I never really saw myself as a goal setter, at least not in the "Napoleon Hill" kind of way. I'm not a visual thinker. I am a verbal thinker. I can't make clear pictures in my head. Nor can I taste or smell things in my imagination. My brain doesn't work that way.

While writing this book I thought about the first motorcycle I bought when I was thirteen and I thought for a moment that maybe I was a goal setter. I wanted that bike and I made it happen. But how?

Ever since I was about sixteen I dreamed of moving to the west coast. I thought about it a lot. When I moved out on my own, I often asked friends if they were interested in going to BC and checking it out. No one was interested and so I just daydreamed about it. At the time I didn't think that I could just pack up and do it alone. But then, when I was twenty-two, it happened almost through no fault of my own I found myself living in Deep Cove in North Vancouver. (It's a long story that happened very quickly... maybe I'll write about it in another book.) the thing is it became a reality.

I used to tell my friends about the kind of woman I was going to marry. They all told me I was crazy and that my standards were too high. They all saw two main problems with my idea. First there was no woman like that out there. Second, even if there was someone who fit the description, she'd have nothing to do with a guy like me. Turns out they were all wrong and when they did meet my wife, they had to eat their words. (*They also wondered if I kept her medicated.*)

Same goes for my Z to A retirement plan. Most people thought it was a stupid idea. How can taking tiny steps actually amount to anything substantial? Well it did.

I guess what I'm trying to say is... to quote Barney Rubble (from the Flintstones) "Think big and be big Fred."

Set lofty goals if you want. Think about them often. Talk about them with friends and family. It doesn't matter whether they believe in you or even whether *you* believe in you. Talking about and thinking about your dreams is the way to keep them alive. I'm not a big write them down kind of a person but, if that works for you, do it.

The important thing to remember is to find a way to take those little steps. Don't focus or worry about how you are going to get to the top of the mountain. Just start climbing. Some of the path will be clear and easy and other parts will be tougher, colder and less smooth. Don't waste your time inventing hurdles and barriers that may never appear, that only keeps you from trying. The idea is to deal with each obstacle as they come.

Maybe you're thinking that there is no way you'll make your dreams come true. That's ok. Maybe your ultimate dream won't come true. It's possible that you'll die before reaching it. There's a possibility that your dream might change along the way too. It's all good.

Think of it this way. If your goal is to climb a mountain because you want to have a better view, start climbing. One step, then another.

A few years into your climb your friends might be shouting up at you, "Hey fool, look at you and your dreams of climbing to the top of the mountain. You've been at it for years and we can still see you. You're no better off than we are."

But you'll know it's not true. You'll be shouting down to them, "Are you kidding me? The view from here is incredible. I've seen the world from where you are and I can tell you the world looks different from up here. I am so much closer to the top and my view changes almost every day. Even if I die here, I will have had the opportunity to take in this beautiful view. My life is so much better because I climbed."

"The hardest part of achieving your dream is to admit you have one."

Chapter Thirteen: Plan U

August 2005 - Up, up and away!

"Don't judge each day by the harvest you reap but by the seeds that you plant." -Robert Louis Stevenson

The day we moved in we started talking about plan U. I'd been looking forward to this part of our lives for a few years; plan U was simple - find a job that would be less hard on my health and hopefully bring in a little more income. The Salvation Army thrift store was killing me in more ways than one. At the time I was dealing with some pretty harsh allergies and working in a lot of mold and mildew wasn't great for my health. I was coughing and wheezing and for the last couple of years I'd been wearing a mask to help protect my lungs.

I had mentioned the idea of quitting my job to the mortgage broker at the time of our interview and he pointed out that it didn't matter what I did *after* I got into the house; as long as I didn't miss a payment everything would be fine. I had already talked to my in-laws about this before they co-signed and they were happy that I wanted to leave and try to work on getting healthier.

As we did with every plan, we started thinking about what little steps I could take to get myself into a new job. In addition to that, I also wanted a place that would offer me opportunities to advance and better my situation.

I asked myself, "What's the least I can do and still be able to say I did something?" The answer was simple: do what I always do, talk to people.

I was prepared to try almost any kind of job. I had a feeling someone somewhere was going to help me find my new career. There was a company out there that needed somebody like me. I was on the lookout. Somehow my need was going to fill someone else's need.

After a few weeks of talking with people I was no closer to finding a new job let alone a lead. Then, one morning I was sitting at my computer looking online to see if anything was available in my area. My biggest obstacle at the time was the unemployment rate. It was high at the time, about 7%. Things weren't looking. I got up and made my way to the bathroom for my morning ablutions.

I sat there for a while and then out of desperation I said to God, "I need out of the Salvation Army. If you need me there for whatever reason I'll stay. But I want you to know, that I know, that you know, that I know, that you know, that I need out."

I made my way back to my computer to continue the search. My Yahoo! Messenger (yes I'm that old) suddenly popped up. The message read, *Send resume, job at Costco.* I called out to the wife and asked her if she talked to anyone that morning. I told her about my plea and the message that just came in. "The Lord works in mysterious ways." she said to me.

My spirits were lifted. I printed out a resume and dropped it off the same day. One, two, three weeks passed by and nothing happened. I was starting to worry that my Costco opportunity might have passed me by. Now it just so happened that the thrift store I worked at had a hair salon. Donna the hairdresser rented part of the store for her beauty parlor. I was responsible for mopping the floors in the store before we opened and Donna and I would often have a chat while she was preparing for the day. One fateful morning she asked me how my job search was going, I told her I was waiting for a call from Costco, "Hopefully." I said. "It's been almost a month."

Donna smiled and nodded her head knowingly, "I'm sure they'll call."

"I hope you're right." I said. She smiled and I continued mopping. On my way back around Donna told me she made a call to Costco on my behalf. I was totally surprised. It turns out that her husband worked at Costco. She called the store and told him to find my resume and give it to the appropriate manager. She told Grant (her husband) to tell them that they should hire me, in fact they needed to hire me. She talked me up and that same day my phone rang. I had an interview.

I could hardly contain myself when I told Tom (the driver of the donation truck and my partner in crime) that I had an interview that week. I told him it would take about 20 minutes. We planned our day and lunch around it. (Thanks Tom!) At one point during the interview the manager asked me what position I was looking for. Suddenly I heard the voice of my step-father Gerry in my ear, "If you really want a job, ask for the job nobody wants."

So, I said to Vallery (the manager), "I want the job nobody wants."

She looked at me a little confused. "What does that mean?"

I said, "I'm sure there's a job at Costco that no one wants to do?"

She said, "Cleaning the bakery."

I said, "That's the job I'm applying for."

Needless to say, (but I will), I got the job. By the end of October I had my new job. It was part-time, but I was making the same amount of money and I only had to work thirty hours a week instead of forty. As I'm sure you guessed, those extra ten hours a week of autonomy were very much appreciated as I got to spend more time with my wife and kids.

Plan U was to get a new job. Mission accomplished. Now if only we could find a way to bring in a few extra bucks. The first thing I did was talk to the bakery manager, he said he had no extra hours to offer me but I could ask the front end manager to see if they need help. It turns out, it was pretty easy to get the extra hours. I called in two or three times a week and as it turns out I got all the hours I wanted.

Our youngest would soon be going to school with her sister and that meant getting invited to birthday parties and outings. Of course that costs money. So we decided it was time for the kids to pull their weight. After all, they were already four and six years old! We got them a paper route.

It's never too early to teach them the value of time and money. Of course they couldn't do it themselves (although at first they wanted to). The papers were on Tuesday, Thursday and Saturday. The route consisted of a hundred and two papers or a twenty minute walk. Sharla did the Tuesday and Thursday papers while the girls were at school. On Saturday the three of them would head out together. Naturally the twenty minute route turned into a one and a half hour route that came complete with a picnic lunch break. Every house on the route had a unique name. There was the "cow candy" house, the "Kim Possible" house, the "kitty cat" house and so on and so on.

They were bringing in a solid twenty-five dollars a month each. We opened a bank account for them and when the birthday parties came around, we'd take them shopping and they would buy presents for their friends. Turns out they always knew what their friends wanted.

As for me, in just under two years I worked my way into a Front-End Lead position. The new position was full-time and bumped me up to the top rate pay scale plus a dollar. It was an incredible twelve dollar an hour raise. Things were looking pretty good.

Once again I was amazed at what tiny little actions could do. I didn't have to change the way I lived, I didn't have to make any serious sacrifices, all I had to do was let people know what I needed. In my life I have been blessed with knowing people who were willing to help me achieve my goals and I have also had the honor of being able to help others. What a blessing it is to help people. Sometimes in life you're the one who needs help and at other times you're giving it out. Some people have a hard time accepting help and to those people I say, "Please don't deny me the opportunity to do good."

I'm sure most of you out there will agree that helping people gives you a good feeling. So why is it that when you need help you can't just let it be?

<u>Side note:</u>

Commit this to memory, no one person can accomplish anything alone. Even if you're a solo artist, you need fans to buy your art. Good things only happen if you ask for help. People who want to help you will help and people who don't want to help won't. It's that easy.

"Work hard, be kind and amazing things will happen." Conan O'Brien

Chapter Fourteen: Success

You don't have to bat a thousand to hit a home run.

"Try and fail, but never fail to try."

-Jared Leto

Fast forward to 2021 with me for a moment, it's about 3 months before we retire from our 9 to 5 work life. Well, more like 8 to 4:30, 12:30 to 9, 10 to 6:30, but you get the idea. Anyhooo...

I'm sitting in the lunchroom with a colleague. He says to me, "It's incredible how you and Sharla keep trying new things. You don't seem to worry about failing or looking like fools; you just keep trying new stuff all the time."

I shrugged my shoulders, "What else are we supposed to do?"

He smiled, "You have no choice but to succeed big at some point."

"What makes you say that?" I asked.

"You guys are always stepping up to bat and swinging. You're playing the odds. At some point you're bound to hit a home run."

"And you don't think that's crazy?" I asked him.

"I think it's great!" he said.

I couldn't help but smile, "Thanks for those words of encouragement. Have you thought about listening to your own counsel?"

"I'm not like you." he said.

"That's where you're wrong." I countered.

"There's no reason to fear failure. The only people who think you're stupid for failing are people who don't try anything new and the odds are they're probably miserable *because* they don't try. The truth is most people are like you and me; we see people who try and try again, as brave and courageous."

Am I worried about looking stupid? Does it bother me when I fail? Do I wish that all my ideas were successful on the first attempt? The answer is yes, yes, and yes. However, I am not going to let a momentary lapse of reason stop me from trying and doing new things.

I constantly have to remind myself to take my own advice. Why is it so hard to take our own advice and encourage ourselves? You'd never tell your toddler they're stupid for failing at anything. You wouldn't call them brainless for trying, but we're so quick to call ourselves mindless, ignorant fools. Let's talk to ourselves like we talk to little children. When things don't go your way, let your inner child know it's ok and give them the pep talk they deserve.

"Staying positive doesn't mean you have to be happy all the time. It means that even on hard days you know there are better days to come." -Anonymous

"Staying positive doesn't mean you have to be happy all the time. It means that even on hard days you know there are better days to come." -Anonymous

Chapter Fifteen: Plan T

January 2007 - Refocusing

"It does not matter how slowly you go as long as you don't stop" - Confucius

By 2007 Plan Z looked way different than its original outline. It was hard to believe that we'd been at this for six years already. How was it possible that all these little steps got us to where we were? It was amazing.

Below is a side by side look at plan Z 2001 and Plan Z 2007.

- 2001 - I Work for minimum wage until I'm 65
  2007 - I Work at Costco at top rate until I'm 65

- 2001 - We rent our whole lives
  2007 - Pay off our mortgage in 25 years (61 years old.)

- 2001 - Raise the kids
  2007 - Raise the kids

- 2001 - We'll be debt free at fifty seven years old.
  2007 - We'll be debt free at forty (hopefully… darn reality)

- 2001 - We'll start saving for retirement at fifty seven, giving us eight years of savings.
  2007 - We are saving for retirement and taking advantage of matches at work. Giving us twenty-eight years to save.

- 2001 - At sixty-five we'll have a few thousand dollars saved up and we collect our pensions.
  2007 - We'll collect our pensions at 65 and have over $200,000.00 in savings.

- 2001 - Over the course of 28 years, we'll spend our spare time writing, creating videos, and art. At sixty-five we can do more of it.
  2007 - All of the above, plus going to concerts and taking a few trips with the kids. At sixty-five we can do more of it.

As I looked back, I was amazed at how little effort it all seemed to take. I felt as if I hadn't really done anything special. How could it be? Our lives were so different from our original Z plan.

I cannot stress enough to myself and to you the reader that it's really and truly all about baby steps. Those of you who've had babies or have seen babies, know that there is a one hundred percent guarantee that the baby will fall many times when she first learns to walk. There is also a very good chance that at some point she will stop falling and success will be hers. The baby will walk. I guess what I'm saying is be a big baby.

In January of 2007 it was time to update our budget. After all, we were now paying for a mortgage, property taxes, water taxes etc. I was also making more money. I needed to find a way to improve on Plan Z, and as per usual, it had to be something small and hopefully easy.

I started by revamping our budget, I was hoping this would spark a new goal to set. One of the first things I did was set up my budget so that I could see what I called our *National Debt* or *Family Debt*. The formula was simple: (Savings) - (Debt including our mortgage). It was a real eye opener. "That's a lot of red ink." I said to my wife.

The good thing about seeing our National Debt was that I knew exactly what our net worth was. I was inspired. Plan T would be turning red ink into black.

I know that budgeting doesn't really sound like something that inspires, but as it turns out, people who budget and buy things on purpose actually feel better about what they have and enjoy life more. I love this quote by Dave Ramsey, "A budget is telling your money where to go instead of wondering where it went."

The first thing you need to remember about budgeting is that it will not limit you. It will have the opposite effect, it will free you to do the things you really want. The first six months will probably be hard, you'll be building new habits. After the adjustment period it gets exciting. Why? Because you see progress and you begin to feel empowered. You go from being a slave to your money, to being the master of it.

Organizing your money doesn't have to be a big chore or complicated. Nor does it have to be boring and depressing. Having a financial plan will give you control. It may be fun to let go of the steering wheel once in a while, but if you don't put your hands back on the wheel, you're going to crash.

Like everything else in life, you're probably going to fall off the wagon as you learn to manage your spending. It's not a reason to give up. With time you'll build good habits and soon you'll be setting aside funds for those unexpected situations. Life is less scary when you have a net below.

One of the most exciting and addictive things about budgeting for me was watching the red sea of debt going down. It didn't matter if it was one dollar or a hundred, it always pumped me up when the red number dropped. It took us several years to reach black ink. I remember that day thinking, if we cashed in all of our RRSPs and stocks we could pay off the mortgage and be completely debt free. Of course we didn't do that but it was nice knowing that we were there.

When I first started budgeting, I used to go over my budget once a week. Every Friday night or Saturday morning I'd sit down and punch in my numbers. Now that we're retired, I go over it once a month.

How should you create your budget? Try different things. I changed the look of my budget almost every year. It's fun. Below is a basic example that I hope inspires you to start.

First you'll need to sit down with your partner and get all your stuff out in the open. Let's say your plan Z is for you and your partner to work at a minimum wage job until you're 65. At 65 you'll get your pension and enjoy reading books and going for walks, work in a garden and watch a few shows before going to bed. This is your life's dream.

Depending on where you are in life and if you can, you'll want to have a few important goals in your Z plan.

1. Try setting a debt free goal. That means no credit card debt, no car payments and if you're lucky enough to have a house, no mortgage.
2. You'll want to have as much savings as possible. This is made easier when you have no debt.

3. It's a good idea to know how much your future life will cost you. Rent, insurances, electricity and any other bills you will probably have. I would suggest using a 4-5% inflation rate. You can find inflation calculators online.

If you find that a 5% inflation rate is too high and intimidating, then use a 3% inflation rate, this is a solid number that is probably more realistic over a long term. I just like using higher numbers because I'd rather overshoot on my projections (that's just me).

If you're not sure how inflation works here's a simple example. From 1914 to 2022 the average inflation rate was 3.02% year over year. According to the Bank of Canada inflation calculator, a basket of goods worth $100.00 in 2000, would cost you $160.00 in 2022. The average inflation rate during that time period was 2.15%.

The reality is not all things follow inflation, some things are more. For example, rent and housing prices have gone way up. Televisions, clothing, phone plans, computers and cars have come down. No one knows what the future brings but we can guess by looking at the past.

Grab a piece of paper or open a new document on your computer and over the next week or two write down the following.

1. How much you owe on every credit card, car loan and line of credit.
    - The interest rate for every card
    - How much money you paid in interest
    - What is your minimum payment?
    - How long will it take you to pay off this debt?
    - Can you do it before you're sixty-five?

2. Write down your mortgage/rent payment
    - How much you pay in interest on your mortgage
    - Will you be able to pay off your mortgage by sixty-five?

3. All other bills, taxes, life insurance, car insurance, food, gas, booze, restaurants, netflix, internet, cable, the list goes on.

Once you have all these things together you'll see where all your money is going. When writing down your plan Z, you'll keep just the basics.

1. Rent/mortgage, city taxes (hopefully you'll be mortgage free by the time you retire)
2. Electricity/Hydro/gas/oil bill
3. Food

These are the things you need to live. A roof, electricity and food. After you have those things down, we'll start to spoil ourselves with a car, cable and other *wants*.

So in the end, plan T was all about updating our budget and seeing exactly where we stood financially. Although it wasn't an automatic improvement to the Z plan, it did help us to stay focused.

Remember that the example above is just an example. You have your own Z plan.

"You can't plan your starting point, but you can plan your finish line."

Chapter Sixteen: Moolah

Money is not a dirty word

"Money is a tool. Used properly it makes something beautiful; used wrong, it makes a mess!" -Bradley Vinson

Tool - *noun.* An implement, especially one held in the hand, as a hammer, saw, or file, for performing or facilitating mechanical operations.

Money - *noun.*   Any article or substance used as a medium of exchange, measure of wealth, or means of payment.

Here are a few tips to help with your money.

1. Pay for your insurance upfront. Most times if you pay monthly, you get charged interest, anywhere from 4% to 35%.

2. Paying your insurance upfront could also get you a discount. We've seen some as high as 8%.
3. Bundle up your insurance. Car, home, life and ask for a discount. Tell the broker you are shopping around and you'll save.
4. Need a car? Do your research and buy pre-owned.
5. The dollar store rarely saves you money in the long run. Pound for pound it's usually more expensive and the quality can be poor.
6. Negotiate. Phone, internet, car, home, interest rates, etc. Every year or so I have a chat with my cell phone company because they want to raise the price of their service. I do some quick research to show them there are cheaper alternatives and let them know that although I appreciate the service, I'm not married to the company. Don't be rude, you'll always do better with an attitude of gratitude. My cell phone bill has gone up $10.00 in 18 years.
7. Collect points. We use our non-credit card points card to collect. Some stores give us one percent, others up to four percent.
8. If you have a high level of self control, shop at Costco. Eat a big breakfast before going shopping. That usually saves me a bundle.
9. Get into gardening. Not only does it save you money in the summers, it helps ground you mentally and it tastes great. The best

part is sharing with your neighbors, friends and family.

10. Use a calculator when shopping. Seeing the number keeps you in line.

11. Check your receipt for double scans or wrong prices before you leave the store. This saves me hundreds of dollars a year. No kidding.

12. Keep an eye on flyers and discounts. I love it when I see 50% off stickers on stuff I can freeze.

13. Don't buy bottled water. Not only is it bad for the environment, it's fucking stupid. You have free water coming out of your tap. Use a water filter.

14. Learn how to invest. Don't go firing your financial advisor until you know what you are doing. Acquire the knowledge you need to invest by studying, and starting slowly. Start with one or two hundred dollars. The fees on ETFs are usually less than a quarter of one percent (0.25%). Mutual funds are between 0.5% to 2% and then there's your financial advisor fees of about 1% or more. The irony is the less money you have the more they charge you.

15. Look for a high interest savings account.

16. Learn about GICs and guaranteed savings.

17. If you get a raise, put that money right into savings. Keep living on what you were making yesterday.

18. Pay off your high interest loans.
19. Do not go into overdraft. Some banks charge you for overdraft protection whether you use it or not. The average interest on overdraft in Canada is 20%.
20. Save, save, save.
21. If your employer has any kind of matching or savings plan, use it and maximize it.
22. If it's broken, clean it. 90% of the time if you clean a 'broken' appliance, it will work.
23. Sell stuff you don't want or need anymore.
24. Pay with cash.
25. Save your loose change. I do this and put away between $500.00-$1000.00 a year, just in time for Christmas.
26. Build an emergency fund.
27. Spend less than you earn.
28. Think of the stuff you buy in terms of hours worked. Is that item really worth 36 hours of your precious time?
29. Cancel subscriptions you don't need. Do you really need two or three streaming services?
30. Don't save your credit card information online. If you have to punch in all those numbers when buying online, you may find yourself just saying forget it.
31. Don't use an ATM that's not your personal bank. You'll be paying fees from both banks.
32. Like to read? Go to the library, you can get digital books there too.

33. Go for walks. You will improve both your physical and mental health. Do it on a regular basis and you may also reduce the amount of prescription drugs you take and lower your overall costs.
34. Ask your pharmacist for the generic version of a drug.
35. Eat at home.
36. Don't pay banking fees. There are plenty of options out there. I haven't paid for personal banking since 1996.
37. Save up and pay cash for that thing you want.
38. Use that senior discount.
39. Eat leftovers.
40. Pay attention to your money.

"Money, it's a hit!" -Pink Floyd

Chapter Seventeen: Plan S

The mortgage. April 2007

"(Burn baby burn) burn that mother down, (Burn baby burn) disco inferno, (Burn baby burn) burn that mother down" -Leroy Green / Tyrone Kersey

I found myself thinking about the mortgage and the twenty-five year plan to pay it off. I'd be sixty-one by the time we were done paying for our place. Don't get me wrong, I was happy to be in the situation I was in. When I thought about our future selves, I dreamed of just paying land taxes once a year instead of rent every month. But still, twenty-five years was a long time.

We learned over the years that just saying we'll be debt free by a certain time doesn't alway make it so. As with everything else in our lives, we found ourselves falling off the wagon and other times the horse and every now and then the wheels fell off the bus. The important thing is that we learned new things each time and we soon became masters of the quick recovery. Even though our goal of being credit card free took us longer than we expected we didn't let that bring us down. We knew that if we just kept moving, one day we'd be there. We never gave up. Instead we refocused and adjusted as needed.

Owning our own home came with a lot of surprises. Land taxes, water taxes, garbage taxes, maintenance and things like that. Who knew my wife wanted to landscape so much? We decided that plan S would be something that could get us mortgage free sooner. After all, we knew the only two guarantees in life were death and taxes. We couldn't control that, but we could control our mortgage payments.

We began writing down and implementing basic ideas. The first step we took was paying off the mortgage every payday or accelerated biweekly. Instead of paying $650.00 once a month, we'd pay $325 every two weeks. This part of the plan was accomplished with a couple of emails. Those three or four emails saved us over three years worth of payments. It also saved us over $12,000.00 in interest. Once again a simple step saved us thousands of dollars.

Doing almost nothing and saving tons of moolah, that is what I call fun. What else could we do to get the mortgage paid off faster? We thought about making lump sum payments, but I quickly realized that wasn't going to work for us. After all, if we had "lump sum" money, it would need to go onto the credit cards first. So, what else could we do?

I thought, hmmm… If I was renting, the landlord would probably raise my rent every year. That would be an increase of anywhere between 2% to 4%. So, I decided I would raise my "rent" every year by 4%. I emailed the bank and asked them to increase our bi-weekly payments by $13.00. Now we'd be paying $338.00. Thirteen dollars a pay seemed very manageable. Doing this every year until the mortgage was paid off would save us another 3 years and about $12,000.00 in interest.

So those two little steps would take our twenty-five year mortgage and turn into a nineteen year mortgage. We could be mortgage free by the time I was fifty-five. That was nuts!

It's important to remember that not all plans are going to work out without a hitch. I know I've said it before but it's worth mentioning again. Life tends to get in the way of your plans once in a while and you have to accept it. Sometimes you may take a step backwards and feel you've lost all momentum. Let's say your car breaks down and you have no choice but to buy another one. That's a huge debt you have to take on. But then a few months later something happens and you're right back on track or maybe even ahead of where you were before the back step. Remember that all is not lost unless you stop moving forward.

"Pay off your debt first. Freedom from debt is worth more than any amount you can earn." -Mark Cuban

Chapter Eighteen: Time vs Money

The question is not how much money, but how much time

"The question shouldn't be, how much money will THIS cost?

It should be, how much of my time am I willing to sell for THIS?"

Most money is the result of you selling your time. When you go to work (whatever that is for you) you're selling your time to your employer or customer. Every time I make a purchase I ask myself, "Am I willing to sell X hours of my life-time to buy this?"

Some things are worth it, like housing, food, hydro, helping the kids, concerts and so on. I find that thinking this way has allowed me to really think about the things that are important to me. This doesn't mean that I only fulfill my "needs" and forgo my "wants". It just means that I really question whether my "wants" are worth selling parts of my life-time for.

When it comes to money it seems, no one ever thinks they have enough of it. I've read stories about billionaires who thought... Maybe, just maybe if I had another billion dollars then I would be happy. Apparently no one *ever* has enough of it. I've heard it said that money doesn't bring happiness, but it allows you to pick your misery. I'm sure that's true to some degree.

The belief that if I had more money then I'd be happy, was a very hard thing for me to let go. I mean it's so easy to believe, more money equals more happiness. Over time I came to realize that I couldn't buy my happiness and in the end it wasn't really what I was looking for. What I really wanted was to have meaning and to be content.

I learned that I could feel neutral, happy or sad and still have meaning in my life. Happiness, like sadness, comes and goes. When I hear people say, "I'm always happy." it makes my ass twitch. You can't always be happy, otherwise how do you even know you're happy? You have nothing to compare it to. I strongly believe we need to stop selling the idea that we must be happy all the time. It's often referred to as toxic happiness. In my personal life right now, I'd say I live 60% of my time at my baseline, 30% happy and the balance is spread out in anxiety, fear and sadness. I'm not saying you can't be happy a lot of the time, but I'm pretty sure people weren't built to be in one continuous state of emotion.

I'm sure you're familiar with the old saying that people on their deathbeds rarely say they wished that they'd spent more time at the office or made more money. They talk about family and wonder why they didn't spend more time with loved ones. What we really need to do is put our want and need for money into a lifetime perspective.

This may sound strange and a little morrose, but there are times when I'm lying in bed and I think about what it would be like if I was dying. I imagine who'd be there and what I'd say to them. When I'm done it makes me appreciate what I have and what is truly important to me. I know that money is important, we need it. I'm just trying to emphasize that in the end, time is really all you truly own in life.

I've read a lot of books and articles about saving money, getting out of debt and retiring rich. Most of it made sense, but a lot of it didn't resonate with me. I was just an average person who worked forty hours a week and didn't have a huge amount of money to put aside. I was lucky to just have money. So the "pay yourself first" and "start your own company, become a real estate mogul and invest yourself into wealth" was not realistic for me at the time. Of course I thought about being rich. Don't we all think about being millionaires when we're young? I was sure that I'd make my first million before I was twenty five.

The reality of it is, I'm just a simple guy who's working on getting by in life. Even as I write this I still live a very simple life. My true goal was never to travel the world on my own jet. All I really wanted to do was go for walks, play in the backyard, take a trip now and again and do what I want to do, when I want to do it. Knowing that allowed me to know how much money I would need to retire. My goal at the time was to sell some of my present life-time to purchase my future autonomous life-time. Once I had reached a set amount I could stop working and get on with my "real life."

You need to ask yourself what it is that you want. Think about how much it's going to cost you and keep working on your plans.

"Let each thing you would do, say, or intend,

be like that of a dying person."

-Marcus Aurelius

Chapter Nineteen: Plan R

One Million Dollars… Sept 2006

"Often when you think you're at the end of something,

you're at the beginning of something else."

Mr. Rogers

For years I believed that a million dollars was the amount of money I needed to retire. Why? I don't know. It just sounded right. It seemed like being a millionaire was the answer to all my life's wants and needs. By the time I reached thirty-six, I was starting to suspect that making a million dollars wasn't going to be as easy as I first thought it would be.

There was something in me that just wanted to see if I could do it. If I was going to be a millionaire by the time I was sixty-five, I had to get a start on it, and soon. After all, I only had twenty-eight and a half years to get it done. I thought, twenty-eight years is a long time, I should be able to manage. I got out my calculator and was hit with the reality that I'd have to save about $35,000.00 a year to make it.

At the time I was making about $15,000.00 net a year. Hmm, not only would I have to make $35K a year to put into savings, I would also have to make the $15K we were living on. It seemed like an impossible mountain to climb. I would have to basically triple my income. I started to think that maybe, just maybe I was over reaching on the R plan a little. What was I thinking?

I got up from my desk and walked to the back door and looked out into the back yard. The kids were out there playing in the little kiddy pool and my wife was working in the garden. Then it hit me that the kids were playing in *our* yard and I was standing in *our* house. We had come so far from our original plan Z.

Unless I won the lottery, plan R wasn't going to happen overnight. I thought back to everything that we'd done over the past five years and told myself that we had twenty-eight years to make plan R happen.

Over the next few weeks I'd get up every morning and make myself a cup of coffee and crunch the numbers. There had to be a way for me to save a million dollars. Maybe a side hustle? I knew this was just another problem that needed solving. If I was going to get this done I'd have to figure out my small steps. I didn't have to puzzle out every step, just the first one. I went back to the budget over and over and just as I was about to give up… I found all this "free" money in the budget. It just wasn't available today. I'd have to work this out starting from the finish line.

My first step was to continue to round *up* my debt and round *down* any possible savings. Building a cushion in my forecasting equation gave me a sense of control. I scratched out a plan R and it looked a little like this.

1. Focus hard on the credit cards and pay them off in ten years. I'd be forty-seven. I would take the payments from the credit cards and put them in a savings account. My payments at the time were $500.00 a month. This meant that once I was debt free I'd have eighteen years to save that same $500.00 a month. I could possibly save $108,000.00 (rounded down to 100K without any interest). Ok, the goal is $1,000,000.00 - $100,000.00 = $900,000.00, I was on my way.

2. If we stayed on track with plan S, we'd have the mortgage paid off by the time I was fifty-five. This would give me ten years of mortgage payments to throw into my savings. By 2024 my mortgage payments would be just over $1,000.00 a month. Calculator please, $1,000.00 X 12 months = $12,000.00 a year multiply that by ten years and we've have another $120,000.00 (no interest added).

Once again I managed to do nothing and I came up with over $200,000.00 of future savings. All I'd have to do is stay the course with my payments, the only thing I'd change is the account the money was going into. I still had $800,000.00 to raise in twenty-eight years but at least I had a starting point.

Now I only have to come up with a measly $29,000.00 a year of extra income. I set my sights on finding a way to $44,000.00 a year. The idea seemed mad. After all, I could only milk so much out of my fictional money tree. The idea of a million dollars seemed so far out of reach. Having the potential of saving $200,000.00 seemed ridiculous too and yet so possible at the same time.

I was sure that it wouldn't be impossible to find another $800,000.00 somewhere in the world. I was determined to find it. Of course I had to find it by taking small simple baby steps. After all, I still wanted my life. I didn't want the goal of making money my life's priority.

I knew reaching my goal wasn't going to be quick and easy. I had to add a few more cogs to my R plan. The next thing I was going to do was turn my part-time job at Costco into a full-time job. After that was figuring out how to get to the top rate of pay as quickly as possible.

According to the Costco employee agreement at the time, it would take me about five years at full-time to reach the top rate and another year on top of that before I would start getting my bonuses. There had to be a better way.

I talked with a few employees and asked how difficult it was to get full-time at Costco and everyone told me it was next to impossible. Everyone I talked to said they'd been there for years and were still working part-time.

I needed a full-time job to speed things up, I wasn't taking no for an answer. I was already calling in and getting as many extra hours as possible, but I was still part-time and missing out on benefits, pension money and RRSP matches. I talked with more and more people trying to figure out if there was a way for me to get a full-time position. I continued getting extra hours on the front end and after a while I got to know all the managers and supervisors on the front end. I noticed that they always needed people to do programs, such as signing guests up with their own membership, promoting their inhouse credit card or upgrading Gold star members to the Executive membership. I took every opportunity to make myself useful and keep myself in demand.

One day one of the front end managers informed me that there was a full time supervisor position available. One of them advised me to apply for it. I applied and after my interview and a couple of great references from two of the managers, I got the job.

Not long after joining the Costco team I was working full-time at top rate plus one dollar. Not only had I reached the top rate in less than the five plus years it would have taken me with the traditional method, but I blew the $44,000.00 a year goal out of the water. I was now bringing in over 50K a year, plus all the benefits like RRSP matches, pension, dental and medical. It all added up to awesome.

I realized during that time that although it was difficult, it wasn't impossible to get full time work at Costco. The problem was that most people didn't want to leave their department to make it happen. It wasn't a lack of opportunity, it was a lack of flexibility.

Soon after my promotion I was having a conversation with one of my co-workers. She said, "I can't believe I've been here seven years and you've been here less than three and you're working full time and making more money per hour than me."

I pointed out that I hadn't done anything that she couldn't do if she just made a few small changes, the first being, applying for different job postings. It took her a couple years to believe in herself but she did it. (Before I retired she'd become one of the best managers I knew and had held over five different positions.)

As I mentioned a few times, Costco had an RRSP matching plan, so as soon as I was eligible I started putting $80 a paycheck into my RRSP and Costco would match 50% up to a thousand dollars a year. They also put (I think at the time it was 2% of my pay) into a Voluntary Pension Plan for me. As an employee I was also able to buy portions of Costco stocks. I started with $10.00 a paycheck.

My retirement savings were growing. The jump to Supervisor was a big one. I went from making $12.50 an hour to $25.00. Instead of living on the new hourly rate, I decided to give myself a $1.00 raise, which was pretty awesome. I was now "living" on $13.50 an hour and since Costco continued to give me raises every year I would increase my "hourly rate" every year.

The rest of my money went into RRSP and debt reduction. Costco was putting about $3000.00 a year into my pension and RRSP every year. The longer I stayed the more they put in. I figured that if we continued investing at the pace we were going and we could get a 4% average return on our money over 26 years that would be around $800,000.00. Holy smokes, we could actually do this. I knew plenty of people who had their 25 year silver badge at Costco, so I knew it was possible for me to do it too.

"A simple fact that is hard to learn, is that the time to save money is when you have some." Joe Moore.

Chapter Twenty

Don't fear the budgets

"A budget tells us what we can't afford, but it doesn't keep us from buying it." -William Feather

I don't have enough money to budget. Budgets are too restrictive. I want to enjoy my life and budgeting means not having any fun. Budgets are too complicated. These and many more excuses can be found in the poor persons handbook.

Let's be honest, most people like budgeting as much as they like a healthy diet and lifestyle. But we need to ask ourselves why? Is it really because it's a waste of time or that it might cramp our "avant garde" lifestyles? I doubt it.

If you want to get ahead in your financial life, the odds are that you are going to need to learn how to budget. You need to know how much money you have and where it's going. This cannot be emphasized enough.

Did you know that budgeting could actually save your relationship? Think about it, the top three reasons marriages end are:

1. Infidelity
2. Death of a child
3. Money

So, ya, it's pretty important to know what you are doing with your money. According to a 2020 Intuit survey, 60% of those surveyed didn't know how much money they spent the previous month. If you look around you'll see plenty of good hard working people who are struggling financially. It's very possible that a lot of people you know are having a hard time making ends meet and you don't see it because they're really good at hiding it.

I've questioned hundreds of people about their personal finances and I've learned that most people don't know where their money goes. They don't know how much debt they have. They don't know how much interest they are paying every month. I've met people who don't even know how much money they have in their primary bank account, let alone any RRSP or savings they might have. All they seem to know for sure is that if they had just a little more money then they'd be happy. A little more money and all their financial woes would go away; that can be true, but rarely is it the case.

When I ask folks why they aren't trying to find solutions to their situation, they try to rationalize it by placing the blame on some financial boogeyman who won't let you get ahead in life. It's the government's fault, if it wasn't for all the taxes. It's the boss's fault for not paying them more.

It's their partner's fault for overspending. It's the bank's fault, because they're charging high interest on overdraft and credit cards.

The basic idea is if it's someone other than me who's responsible for my misery, then I can't fix it. I have no choice but to be miserable and live with it. The previous statements may seem ridiculous to you, but you'd be amazed at how many people think this way.

I remember having a chat with a friend. He was telling me how he could barely afford to eat after paying the bills and that he was using his credit cards to stay alive. I found it kind of curious because he had a habit of buying the most expensive cheeses and top of the line steaks. At one point I asked him how much he paid for his monthly cellphone bill. As it turns out he was paying over $180.00 a month for his plan. I mentioned that it seemed a little steep. He told me it included the phone. "Wow, a cracked screen phone is expensive nowadays." I jested.

"It wasn't cracked when I got it." he said. My attempt at sarcasm went unappreciated.

I went on to tell him that I paid $142.00 a month. He nodded his head in approval. I told him that it was for four lines, unlimited calling, texting and 2 Gb of Data. He laughed and told me he could use up 2Gb of Data over lunch. "You must be really important, does using all that Data earn you money?" I asked.

He sneered.

"Wouldn't you rather spend $35.00 a month on a phone and not go into debt?" I asked.

"Whatever!" was his response, "I wouldn't be caught dead with a cheap phone like yours and no Data." I reminded him that I had 2GB.

All I was trying to do was point out the ridiculousness of his made up situation. He was buying expensive food items and over paying for his phone. All the while complaining that he was dirt-poor and flat broke and wasn't getting paid enough to do this job.

If you're reading this, I suspect that you're thinking hard about your future and want to make some changes to increase your odds of having a good life free from as much debt as possible and that you want to increase your chances of a brighter future and a higher quality of retirement living than the one you're in line for.

I'm not going to say that budgeting is the only way to financial freedom. I will say that it's the best way I know of. If you are like the majority of people living with a moderate income, budgeting can save your ass.

Remember that we're all in this for the long haul. This isn't a get rich quick scheme. First we build a realistic plan Z, one that shows us where we might end up if we change nothing. Then we improve on that plan step by step. The goal is not to retire tomorrow, it's to plan for a retirement that is better than the one we're heading for.

"Budgeting isn't about limiting yourself, it's about making the things that excite you possible." - Anonymous

Chapter Twenty-One: Plan Q

Q is for emergency 2008

"No one sees a recession coming." -

Anonymous

With the long term plan R in the works things were looking pretty good. That is until September of 2008 when the Dow Jones industrial average fell 777 points. It was the largest single-day loss in its history. Within a few days everybody was panicking; even people who had no money in the markets were losing their shit.

Most of my friends were starting to talk about possible layoffs. I was like, "Damn, I just got my shit together and now the world is going to come crashing down on me? Sounds about right."

I had to calm my shit down, I was freaking out. Over the past three years I had managed to save up a few bucks and overnight I had lost 40% of those savings. I'd been buying Costco stocks through payroll and the stock price was cut almost in half. This was going to be the end of me. All my plans for nothing, I was going to have to find a new job, work my way back up, my kids would be shoeless, my wife would leave me... "My God, my

God, why have you forsaken me?" Ok, that might be a little dramatic, but you get the jist.

For a couple of weeks my anxiety was through the roof as all kinds of rumors, falsehoods and alternative facts were flying around spreading like wildfire. Everyone everywhere was talking about the coming armageddon. Finally I sat down with my wife and said, "Whatever happens happens. We'll be fine, we'll make it work, we'll figure it out."

This is when we realized that we needed an emergency plan. Shit happens and we need to be as prepared as possible for it when it hits the fan. Plan Q was pretty much a stand alone plan, it was all about preparing for the worst. What would we do if I got laid off or lost my job? Plan Q was something I could and would return to. It was our emergency fire plan. It's something you hope you never need, but you're happy you have it when you do.

1. We would call the bank and have them reduce our bi-weekly payments to our original payments.
2. I would start looking for a job right away.
3. Our credit card payments would go to minimum payments plus interest.
4. We would find ways to tighten the budget even more and spend as little as possible for the next while.

We decided to put most of the plan into action right away and keep an eye on world events. For the next few paychecks we left the mortgage payments where they were and we just paid minimum payment plus interest on our credit cards. We quit drinking and cut back on miscellaneous spending. Everything else went into the bank so we could have some funds if and when things fell apart. All we could do now was hold on and wait for the other shoe to drop.

At first I thought plan Q had nothing to do with my retirement, but I soon realized that I had many years ahead of me before I retired. This wasn't going to be the last time I would face possible disaster. There are wars, market crashes and as we found out in 2019 pandemics and more bear markets. We can't prepare for all the unforeseen events in our lives. But we can create a plan that covers our asses for a few months. The important thing is to have some kind of plan and then readjust when we see a storm coming like a hurricane or when one hits us like an earthquake.

The firemen in commercials used to say, "If you're ever on fire, Stop, Drop and Roll." That's some sound advice. I use it during times of panic to remind myself what to do.

S - Stop.
T - Take a deep breath.
O - Observe the situation.
P - Practice what I preach.

D - Doctor the plan if and when needed.
R - Realize it / make it happen.
O - Overhaul the plan if necessary.
P - Persist and adapt.

R - Rest.
O - Observe.
L - Live.
L - Look for the light at the end of the tunnel.

The most important part of stop, drop and roll is being able to adjust, readjust and possibly scrap it all and start a new plan if absolutely necessary.

Funny thing is when my wife and I retired back in 2021 the market was doing pretty good. Then in January of 2022 things started to fall apart in the market. At the time of writing this in October of 2022 the DOW was down -20.95%, NASDAQ -32.40 and the S&P 500 was -24.77% from their highs.

Before we retired a few people had asked what I'd do if the market crashed right after we retired. How would we manage? I told them that we didn't want to live on "what ifs". I told them that we were preparing for all kinds of scenarios. Since we did have the majority of our money in the markets we decided to put aside three years worth of living expenses. We figured if the market did crash, we'd have three years for it to recover. We also assured them that we'd be willing to return to work, if things got too expensive or we were running out of money. Our worst case scenario at the time was that we'd have to work an average of eight hours a week at minimum wage each to make ends meet.

As it turns out we helped our friends paint a couple of apartments the year we retired and the extra income came in handy. We worked about four weeks in total that year (getting paid a decent wage) and as it happens it worked out to being the eight hours a week (at minimum wage) we had planned on.

When the market came down in 2022, we didn't panic too much. We knew we had three years in our life fund. Inflation went up, but so did our savings interest rates. The higher interest rates added to our monthly passive income stream. The other major source was our dividend payments which we reinvested.

Will three years of savings be enough? Only time will tell. Our goal is not to spend our entire life fund, it's to add to it. We're slowly switching our investment portfolio from a hold and grow to a dividend paying portfolio with the hopes of living off the dividend payments and adding to our life fund.

"As sure as the spring will follow the winter, prosperity and economic growth will follow a recession." - Bo Bennett

Chapter Twenty-Two

One step forward

"If you can't fly then run, if you can't run then walk, if you can't walk then crawl. But whatever you do, you have to keep moving forward."

- Martin Luther King Jr.

Every little step you take will get you closer to your destination. Don't worry that one step doesn't seem to make a difference, just know that it does. One step seems like nothing, until the day you look back and see how far those steps have taken you.

Keep in mind that Failure x Repetition = Success. If you haven't failed it's only because you haven't tried. Could you imagine if babies stopped trying to roll over because they failed a few hundred times? They would never roll over. Did you know that 12 to 19 month-olds average 2,368 steps a day and fall 17 times per hour? How long would it take you to quit, if you failed 17 times an hour?

Would you ever tell a child to stop trying just because they failed once or twice? Then why do we tell ourselves to stop? Failure x Repetition = Success, don't forget it. I can honestly say that I have failed a thousand times more often than I've succeeded. Sometimes failure is relatively painless, other times it can break your heart. The trick is to learn from it and move on. There are worse things than failure, one is accepting it.

A few chapters ago I talked about lowering your credit card interest rates. Did you try? Did you fail? If so, that's ok. Wait a week and try again. You'll find that after a few attempts you'll get more comfortable making the calls. After a while they'll either reward you for your efforts or you'll have made a few new friends at the credit agency, and if you have a friend at the credit card agency, they'll probably be happy to help you out.

Some things are worth repeating. Here are a few things I'd tell myself as I looked to pay down my credit card debt.

1. I will use my cards as little as possible.
2. The least I will pay is minimum payment plus interest.
3. I will make a payment every payday.
4. I will pay off the lowest dollar amount card first. (I liked the feeling of having a win under my belt.) **Please note:** *If the lowest card you have is going to take you years to pay off, I would go with a high interest card first.)*

5. When I finish paying off a card I will cancel it. I will only keep one card.
6. When I finish paying off one card, I will take that payment and add it to the next card.

The most important thing is to find the method that best fits your needs. You need to have something that will work for you. When times get tough and you feel like quitting, remind yourself why you are doing what you're doing. If you fail or fall back in any way, don't see it as a reason to quit and give up. Take a deep breath, forgive yourself and start again.

"Life is like riding a bicycle.
To keep your balance you must keep moving."
-Albert Einstein

Chapter Twenty-Three: Plan P

Most times… things are going to be ok

"Know what you own, and know why you own it." – Peter Lynch

By Christmas time the Costco head office wrote a letter to the staff letting us know that the company was in good hands, their finances were solid and we had nothing or at least very little to worry about.

There were a few layoffs but they were very short lived. I was worried I might be on the cutting board but as it turned out the cuts didn't go that deep. I breathed a sigh of relief. It turned out that when people needed to save money they shopped at Costco.

One afternoon in early October, I was having my lunch at work. The TV was on and Prime Minister Stephen Harper was on the news. He said something that he got ripped for; he said, "I think there are probably some gains to be made in the stock market. That's my own view."

The Liberal's Dion said, "...he's completely out of touch with reality."

NDP leader Layton said, "I think Canadians are looking for a government that's going to take this issue more seriously than that, and not be so cavalier or so casual."

The truth is, he was right. It was a great buying opportunity. Warren Buffet said something like, "When people are happy, sell. When people are sad, buy." In hindsight Mr. Harper was right. Whether you like the guy or not, it was good advice and the fact that he's got a master's degree in economics… I heeded it.

My investments were down about 40% and that didn't feel too good, but I knew I had a couple of decades to recover it all back. Was there something I could do to take advantage of this crash? The only thing I really knew about investing at the time was buying mutual funds and I felt like I needed to do more than that, therefore I thought about it for a few days.

I told my wife the good news, "I'm not getting laid off." She was happy to hear that.

"So what do we do now?" she asked me. "We don't need to implement plan Q. Do we change it?" I told her we'd keep it on file for the next emergency.

Over dinner we came up with our plan P. The idea was to take advantage of a great opportunity in a time of crisis. I guess this time P was for *Place your bets.* The P plan was to invest. For the next three months we'd continue to pay the minimum payment plus interest on the credit cards and we'd use the extra money to buy Costco stocks.

Like the rest of the market the Costco stock had crashed, losing about 40% of its value. We knew the company was in good hands, which made buying the stock feel less risky. Another great thing was that the Canadian dollar was at par with the US dollar, a rarity for our currency. I asked payroll to increase my stock purchases for the next few paychecks and I held on for the ride.

I told a few friends what I was doing and all but one thought I was crazy. I suggested that they might want to buy a few stocks themselves. No one took my advice… not that I blame them. After all, I barely knew what I was talking about.

After six paychecks I lowered my purchases to $75.00 a pay and we went back to putting full payments on the credit cards. Over the next decade I watched as my Costco investment continued to grow at an average rate of 14% per year.

"The stock market is filled with individuals who know the price of everything, but the value of nothing." — Phillip Fisher

Chapter Twenty-Four

Yes you can

*"A single tiny step you actually take
is better than any big plan left undone."*
-Jane Lee Logan

If things start to feel a little overwhelming, remind yourself that you're not creating some grand master plan; you're just making small improvements on your original Z plan. Those little improvements will morph your Z plan into something newer, something better than what you had before.

It's important that you continue moving forward. Put on your thinking cap and hash over some ideas with the people around you. Once you have a solid idea, take action right away. As soon as you accomplish a step, start working on the next one. There are times when a plan will just jump out at you and other times it may take a few weeks to come up with something new. The trick is to keep thinking about it. Oftentimes I will brainstorm with people and we'll come up with the craziest ideas. A few days later when my brain has had time to let those crazy ideas ruminate, *POW!* A new idea.

Every now and then you may feel discouraged that you can't come up with a new improvement to your plan. Don't get distressed. Your subconscious will work on it while you sleep, eat, play video games etc… It's almost unavoidable, a new goal will emerge. The idea is to keep working your way down the alphabet and sooner than you think you'll find yourself looking into the eyes of your retirement day.

I can't stress enough the importance of moving forward on an imperfect idea. If you wait until your idea is flawless and bulletproof, you'll probably never forge ahead. I've tried to keep all my moves as simple and achievable as possible. I also like to remind myself on a regular basis of what really makes me happy and what it is I'm working for.

As you know by now, I am motivated by "free autonomous time", so when I have a hard time getting excited about executing an idea, I think about how it's going to give me more free time. For example, when I was worried about making the calls to credit card companies I thought, if I can save $1,000.00 in interest payments, that'll save me over a hundred hours of labor. I am buying my future self "free time" and that motivates me.

Look, it's all well and good to make plans and stay motivated about your Z plan, but you also need to know that retirement isn't just about not working. You also need to think about your happiness in retirement. Most of your life is what you make of it. The truth is if you're not happy with life now and you think that retiring is going to make you happy, you're in for a bad surprise. If you want a good retirement the first thing you should do is work on your relationships with yourself and with your family and friends. What is life without family and friends? For 99% of the people out there retiring all alone is not going to make for a happy retirement.

Here's something interesting I read the other day. According to Daniel Kahneman in his essay The Focusing Illusion, if everyone had the same education, the inequality of income would be reduced by less than ten percent. If everyone had the same income, the differences among people in life satisfaction would be reduced by less than five percent. Basically he found that life is what you make of it.

"The happiness of those who want to be popular depends on others; the happiness of those who seek pleasure fluctuates with the moods outside their control; but the happiness of the wise grows out of their own free acts." - Marcus Aurelius

Chapter Twenty-Five:
Plan O

Two upgrades or not two upgrades?

"If the plan doesn't work, change the plan, not the goal."

 Both kids were now in school. Sharla now had more free time to work on the home improvements she had been wanting to do. With me working and Sharla helping at school, we found ourselves in need of a second vehicle and with all the house work she'd been doing we thought a truck would be the best investment.

 After much debate, we decided to buy a pick up truck. Over the last little while we'd been borrowing our neighbor's van and my buddy's truck to pick up our renovation supplies. We figured it would be useful to have our own truck. Since we didn't have the cash on hand to pay for one we decided to buy off the lot and get a loan. The cost was $100.00 every two weeks for 8 years. Our plan was to keep the truck for four years. We figured this would give us enough time to finish all the renos and landscaping. We would then sell the truck and pick up a small car.

Plan O was to upgrade our vehicular situation. As it turns out, Plan O was going to be a little more than just a pick-up truck. One day, I came home from work and my wife was in the middle of redesigning Plan O. "We need a mudroom." she said as I walked in the door with my muddy boots and wet jacket.

"We don't *need* a mudroom." I said as I tripped over her boots. I made my way through the living room dripping water all over the floor. I hung my drenched jacket on the back of a chair. The front door opened. The kids came in and immediately undressed. They threw all their wet clothes in the ten square foot entryway. The pile of clothing not only blocked access to the front door but also denied us a clear passage to the stairs leading up to the second floor.

"We need a mudroom." she repeated. "There is no way I'm going through another wet westcoast winter without one."

I listened as I watched our daughters climbing over the mountain of jackets, boots and ski-pants strewn all over the floor. I noticed a slow moving stream of water making its way to the living room. "Ok, we could use a mudroom." I confessed. "But I can't justify spending tons of money on a seventy-five square foot addition."

She stared at me, "There's no place to even put a hook up and you have to travel halfway through the house to get to the nearest closet. We need to do something." she said. "What if we get a mudroom and add a media-room along with it?"

I was starting to panic a bit. I felt we might be going down the wrong path. After all, the truck was already adding $200.00 a month to our bills. I couldn't imagine what an addition was going to cost us.

I really wanted to stay the course. I didn't want to increase the amount of time it would take to pay off the mortgage and the credit cards. But I also realized that she was right. Sharla had made many sacrifices over the years and never complained. If she wanted a mudroom, she'd get a mudroom.

Over the next few weeks we hashed out the details of plan O. The main goal was to build equity without extending our overall debt payment timeline. If it was possible, we would do it.

Sharla had already spent a few weeks making calls and getting quotes from contractors. In the end we decided to add about four hundred square feet to our home in the form of a mudroom and media room. This was going to add about $60,000.00 to the mortgage. We immediately increased our biweekly mortgage payments by $100.00, which happened to be the amount of money we were getting for our paper route. This would allow us to stay on course and have the house paid off by the time I was fifty-five.

About a month before the renovations were set to begin Sharla decided to get a seasonal job at Costco. She would work the morning shift from 5am to 10am. I would send the kids off to school and she'd be home in plenty of time to welcome them back in the afternoon.

We quit the paper route which meant I no longer had to work seven days a week. Sharla would work both seasonal periods, one from May to Sept and the other from late October to the end of December. As it turned out, the seasonal work would pay for the truck, the addition and allow us slightly increase our payments on the credit cards.

Within two months of starting at Costco the job became a permanent part-time position. The good news continued. Sharla was now able to invest in RRSP, VPP and purchase Costco stocks. Also with both of us working we now had 100% health benefit coverage.

I would have never imagined that buying a truck and building an addition on our home would increase our cash flow and our retirement savings. There were a few bumps in the road of course, but in the end, we managed to get it done.

"A goal without a plan is just a wish." - Antoine de Saint-Exupery

Chapter Twenty-Six

Create a debt free club

"Want to be debt free?

Underestimate your income and overestimate

your expenses"

Debt, it sucks. No one likes it, yet 70% of Canadians are in debt. Total household debt in Canada is over $2,700,000,000.00 (that's over two point seven trillion dollars). Who owes the most? People aged between forty-six and fifty-five. Seniors tend to be the most debt free people in the country. Ok, so if no one likes debt, why do so many of us bathe in it?

There are a few reasons why people are in debt, some are obvious, we spend more than we make. We buy things we don't need. We have easy access to credit and we see credit as free money. We don't want to save up for something we want (That's called instant gratification.) There are also personal tragedies. I had gotten into debt for all the reasons above and when our daughter died of cancer, we lived off welfare and our credit cards for a year.

My biggest problem was mostly that I was a spender and I didn't really think about the purchases I made. For example when I bought something on credit, I didn't think of it as a $500.00 purchase. I thought about it as a $15.00 a month repayment plan and what's $15.00? What I didn't think about was how long it was going to take to pay back that initial $500.00. I didn't spend much time reflecting on all the interest I'd be paying out. I certainly didn't think about whether or not I'd still want the "thing" I bought two years down the road. The truth is I have often bought a "something" and two years down the road I no longer had that thing, but was still paying for it and would be for years. Like many of you I had plenty of reasons and excuses for being in debt. Mostly excuses.

It wasn't until I started thinking about my future that I realized how enslaved I was to the credit card companies and the banks. Why would the banks give someone like me so much credit? At first I blamed the credit card companies for my debt. It took a while for the reality of my situation to register in my brain. Eventually I had to admit to myself that no one had forced me to apply for credit cards or buy things I didn't need or even pay banking fees for that matter. I had to take responsibility for my actions. I finally understood that becoming debt free was not an option but a necessity.

I thought about all the justifications I'd made over the years for being in debt. I decided that for every excuse I had for being in debt I would create a reason for getting out of debt. I needed to change my perspective on my debt. Now instead of focusing on debt creation, I would concentrate not only on debt reduction, but wealth building or as I like to call it, "Buying Future Time". I knew that I couldn't move in two opposing directions at the same time. I had to choose where I wanted to go. So, I set my GPS to a specific address "freedom from debt."

This change in mindset had an impact in the real world. It was all about moving from red ink to black ink. It wasn't easy, but eventually we did it. By the way, it didn't happen overnight.

I'm not ashamed to admit that I live with the fear of failure. Whether it's writing a book, creating a podcast, making videos, making bad investment decisions, staying retired and the list goes on... I get through it by reminding myself that:

(F x R = S) Failure x Repetition = Success
And that F x R is in itself a Success

Some days it's difficult to believe it, especially when I'm in the middle of failure. When those days come, I go for a walk, talk it out with my wife, sometimes I'll listen to a motivational speech or read about other people's struggles and eventual successes. Other days I look back at my past failures and remember how some of them led me to victory.

Based on my personal research I found that people who take actions to reduce their debt usually succeed in reducing it. Problems arise when we miss a short term goal or our debt goes up from the previous month. A lot of people tend to just throw up their hands and call it quits. But we don't have too.

If you want to improve your body and you start going to the gym every day I can almost guarantee you will see a difference in your body at some point. It may not be the first week, but after six to eight weeks, you will see a change. If you quit the first time you miss a day, nothing will change. It's the same with debt reduction. After a few months of seeing your debt go down you'll start to feel pretty good.

Like working out you may decide to cheat, maybe you treat yourself to a little something. The best thing to do is to acknowledge that it might happen. Yes, you may cheat on your budget, but knowing you might, can increase your will power. The trick is not, *not* falling, the trick is getting back up.

Another good tip is sharing your goal with others. By verbally announcing it to friends and family, you are more likely to want to come back with positive updates. Share your success stories with the people in your life. And just as importantly, share your failures and how you plan to learn from them going forward. Of course if the opportunity arises, share the knowledge you've picked up and help others.

Why is it that we rarely hear people brag about how they just paid off a credit card? Yet it's fine to encourage people to go into debt. God forbid you would encourage people or help them reduce their debt and increase their wealth. It seems if you do talk about it you're just bragging (in a bad way). It appears that it's better to help your friends get *into* debt, then have them think about how to get *out*. Seriously? Please let's help each other get over this taboo of money talk.

We need to talk about debt and debt reduction the same way we talk about saving 50% on a piece of clothing we just bought. Instead of adding $50.00 to your debt, you saved 50% and only added $25.00 to your credit card debt. Wow! Good for you! NOT!

We need to get our friends together and encourage them and help them get out of debt. Get together and treat it like a game night. Get all your bills together and come on over. We're going to have a debt free party. My hope is that those who desperately need it, will come join us.

How does a debt free party work? First we just admit that we all have debt and that we're here to help and encourage each other. Some of us will have more debt than others and that's ok, we're not here to shame each other. It's kinda like AA. "Hi, my name is Chip and I'm in debt."

I've been talking about my personal journey of debt reduction/wealth building with my friends and family for years. At first it was hard, I was a little embarrassed and then when I was starting to have some real success, I felt like I was bragging. I was just so excited about getting out of debt I wanted everyone to feel this good. The hard truth is that there are a lot of people who simply don't want to go there. They are "happy" in their debt misery.

After a while, a couple of people started opening up to me and asking me questions. I was happy to brainstorm with them and come up with ideas they could use. I always told people that if I could do it, so could they.

In the last year or so half a dozen people contacted me to let me know they'd paid off all of their credit cards. Some had no debt at all. Others told me how my advice on saving $10.00 a paycheck and slowly increasing over time had amounted to thousands of dollars for their nest egg. They were all starting to build their savings and felt great about it. They were so proud of themselves. They told me that it was hard at first, but it got more and more exciting as their debt decreased and savings increased. They found themselves finding a way to add more money to the bill and eventually it was at zero. They told me that my constant talk about debt reduction, building money reserves and my retirement goals, was the biggest motivating factor. They figured that if I could do it, there was no way in hell they couldn't. And they did, and so can you.

Go out and build your debt free party group. Start your own Debts Anonymous Club. Be there for each other and stop living with the imaginary fear that you can't do it. Together we can.

"One of the best gifts you'll ever give yourself is being debt free."

Chapter Twenty-Seven: Plan N

What if I didn't have to sell so much of my time?

"All we have to decide is what to do with the time that is given us."
-J.R.R. Tolkien

For the next year and a half we just stayed the course. The addition got built, we painted a few rooms and went to work. Things were going pretty good for us, Sharla was working about twenty-five to thirty hours a week and I was putting in my forty. We had updated our budget to include payments for the truck and the addition and we were maxing out on all the matches Costco had to offer. We thought we'd just ride this wave for as long as possible… But of course it wasn't that long until we realized we needed more time with each other.

I was working forty-nine weeks a year and Sharla was working fifty, we got lucky enough to have one day off a week together and two weeks of vacation time in the summer, but that just wasn't enough for us. We decided that plan N would be all about finding a way to get more free time. How on earth would we manage that? We weren't about to quit our jobs. I suggested that Sharla could quit her job, after all we could tighten the budget and live on one income again. That said, we kinda liked the money we were saving and spending. There had to be a better way!

For as long as I can remember with every job I've ever had, I've used up all of my vacation time in the summer months. Summer is the best. I love waking up in the morning and having coffee in the backyard, cutting the grass and just relaxing. Mostly I loved not having to go to work. As I mentioned, I had three weeks of vacation time a year and Sharla had two. The thought of working forty-nine and fifty weeks a year just to get a few off to ourselves wasn't looking that appealing anymore. We decided to change the situation. What were we going to do?

Lucky for us working at Costco had many benefits, one of them was being able to take up to six weeks off in the months of January, February and March. Of course this was an unpaid leave of absence. Plan N was all about finding a way to take those six weeks off. All we needed to do was figure out how. That being the case we took another look at our budget. We knew the priorities were the mortgage, the truck and credit cards.

Since we were on a HELOC, we did have access to our home's equity, but that could easily turn into a fiasco if we weren't very clear with our objectives. We were unquestionably nervous about taking six weeks off. We weren't sure what was going to happen. Were we going to spend more money because we had all this free time?

The first year we decided to test the waters with a four day weekend. Therefore every week in January, February and March was a three day work week. If you're wondering if it was worth it… I'm here to tell you it was. It's crazy how fast that winter went by. By the end of March we had already decided to do it again the following year.

Things worked out pretty even. Our electricity bill went up a little, but our car gas bill went down. As it turns out not going to work everyday cut back on our grocery bills too. The temptation of buying something as we left work was gone. We ended up saving a few hundred bucks there too.

The second year we changed it up a little and we did one week on and one week off. The third year we took every other day off. After that we took the whole six weeks off every year until we retired. For the last few years we ended up having six weeks in January, February and March. We broke up one week of our vacation time and had a four day weekend in April, May, September, October and November. We had nine days off in June and July. In August we had eighteen days off. To say that we had it good is an understatement. Thank you Costco. After a few years we were both getting our bonuses and we just put that money aside and it was more than enough to cover the time off. Our retirement, savings and debt reduction goals were all met and exceeded.

I try to live by the saying, "You can always make more money, but you can't make more time." Those six weeks of winter holidays along with my five weeks of summer holidays (by the time we retired) were awesome. It was like mini retirements.

The craziest part of all this is that many of our co-workers couldn't understand how we were managing all this time off. They all had the same opportunity. There were a few who took full advantage of it, I'd say it was less than three percent of the staff that took advantage of any of the time.

How about you? Can you find a way to buy yourself one day a month? How about one day every three months or even a day a year? What would you do with that special day? It's not that hard to figure out. Let's say you get paid every two weeks, if you're making $16.00/hr your take home would be about $950.00. That means that you get paid around $100.00 a day (take home).

If you set aside $25.00 a paycheck, you could buy yourself one day of free time every two months. If you put aside $10.00 paycheck you could buy yourself a day off every five months. I know some of you reading this will be thinking that two days off a year extra isn't all that great, however that's two days you own. That's sixteen hours you don't have to sell to someone. Trust me, once you start buying your own time back, you'll see that it's worth it and you'll probably find a way to buy even more.

Plan N was all about buying back our time. We took every opportunity to enjoy the benefits that came from hard work and good budgeting. Taking all that extra time off was a great motivator and it encouraged us to keep planning for retirement.

"We all think we have time, you know. It's this miracle substance and there seems to be so much of it, and then all of a sudden, it's gone." - Eloisa James

Chapter Twenty-Eight

Give yourself an allowance

"You're never too old to have little spending money."

Allowance [uh-low-uhns]
Noun
A set amount of money allotted or granted to a person on a regular basis, as for personal or general living expenses.

We were working hard, raising kids and doing a few side art jobs to keep the home machine moving as smoothly as possible. But spending all our hard earned money on bills and necessities and having none for pleasure, was becoming a recipe for disaster. After all, there's more to life than just work and sleep. We wanted to make sure we were able to enjoy our free time.

After a few months of successfully paying the bills and seeing our debt go down a little, we decided to reward ourselves. We bought stuff. A bottle of wine, some special food, a couple of DVDs, stuff we wouldn't normally buy.

Hey, we deserved it. At first, the idea of rewarding ourselves was a welcomed bonus to our lives. We were doing pretty good with our goals. Spoiling ourselves a little didn't seem out of the question. That is until we realized that we were "spoiling" ourselves on a regular basis. All of a sudden we were more focused on rewards than debt.

Our focus was just on our present selves and we forgot all about our future selves. It didn't take too long to grasp the idea that we were heading down a dangerous road. We had to find a happy medium. We live in the now and we wanted to enjoy the now. After all, no one knows how long they have to live. We wanted to enjoy today, while planning for the future.

One thing that helped a lot was that every six months we'd sit down and take a deep dive into our finances and adjust our budget where necessary. We'd look and see where we were with our goals. We'd analyze our successes and our failures. We discovered that the first few months of me taking over the finances went well, but then... (because I'm a spender and love now time) we started rewarding ourselves a little too much.

We needed a way to stay on track and keep ourselves motivated. We sat down and talked about it over the next few days. We decided that spending on pleasure was important. So from now on we'd give each other a set amount of money every payday. Let me tell you, it wasn't much. But it was affordable.

Ten dollars. Yup that was our first allowance. Every two weeks we'd both get ten dollars and with that ten dollars we could do whatever we wanted. Usually one of us would buy a bottle of the cheapest booze with the highest alcohol content. Then the next week the other would do the same. Every Friday night, we'd put the kids to bed and have a little date night. It wasn't much, but you know what? It was ours and it was paid for.

By the time we retired our allowance had risen to a hundred dollars every two weeks. It was a far cry from the ten dollars I used to give myself. Truth be told, I had a hard time spending it all some months. Not the ten dollars, the hundred.

"Give to others, but don't forget to give to yourself too."

Chapter Twenty-Nine: Plan M

2015 The Last Credit Card Payment

"The best thing money can buy is freedom from worrying about money." - Anonymous

In 2011 we celebrated the ten year anniversary of our Z plan. Even though we were the same people our Z plan had changed a lot and so had our lives. Our debt was going down every month and our savings were going up. Our Z plan was almost unrecognizable, much like our children, the plan was growing up too.

We'd taken a few trips back east to see family, and we enjoyed the thrill of going to concerts and staying in hotels. We were thrilled that we could take our kids with us once in a while. We knew that life was about more than just saving up money and paying bills. That said, it was also important that we paid cash for our adventures. If any of our plans made our "national debt" rise, we would wait until we could afford it.

We were pretty blessed. A few months into 2011 we projected that we could reach our financial goals three years earlier than planned. If Sharla continued working and we stayed the course, we could retire at sixty-two.

The next few years went by and we had basically stopped at plan N. Things were moving along nicely and we were pretty happy with our situation. As Sharla and I got raises we added to our savings and continued to pay down debt. Twice a year I would adjust our retirement date. By the time 2015 came along we were planning on retiring at sixty. It was hard to believe we had taken five years off of our Z plan.

We floated on plan N for four years. In January of 2015 we decided it was time to improve plan Z once more. We realized we were still paying way too much in interest on our debts including our mortgage. Things were good, but why were we giving away all this money to our banks? We could use that interest money to buy ourselves more time. We wanted to find a way to pay off all our credit cards with one caveat, we didn't want it affecting the concerts and trips we were taking. It was very important for us to have great experiences with our kids while they were still young.

We thought about it for a while and within a few weeks we came up with a plan. We decided to sell the truck. Most of the big renos were done and we really didn't need a truck anymore. Our eldest daughter was getting her driver's license and we decided that an old used car would be better for her to learn in than our "newer" truck.

A friend of mine had a 1995 Sunfire sitting in his driveway for a while, so I made him an offer. Two hundred and fifty bucks and a DVD player with surround sound. He was happy to get rid of the car and I was happy to get it. I spent a few weeks doing some minor repairs and made sure the car was running. Once I was satisfied with the state of the car we went to Costco and had four new tires put on it. Our new 1995 Sunfire/family car was ready for its new driver.

Needless to say that our daughter was a little disappointed she wasn't going to be driving the truck and asked me why we couldn't just keep it. I told her that I would be fine with her ruining a $250 car, but not so much a $17,000.00 truck.

We'd had the truck since 2009 and lucky for us it held its value rather well. We sold the truck for $11,500.00. We had a balance owing of $4,700.00 which we paid off right away. The truck had turned out to be a pretty good deal. Over the span of six years we ended up paying just under $240.00 a month for the use of the truck. I thought that was a pretty good deal.

We went to the bank and paid off the $4,700.00 we owed on the truck. We got home and thought about the remaining $6,800.00. As it happened we had one credit card left to pay off. The balance was $6,700.00. I logged into my bank account, took a deep breath and made one final payment.

Yes, it hurt real bad. There were so many things we wanted to do with that money, but once we clicked "pay bill" a huge sense of relief came over us. I looked at my wife and said, "Never again. We will never pay another dime in interest again on a card."

That was the last time I ever paid interest on a credit card. We took the extra hundred dollars we had left and went to the liquor store. I bought a nice bottle of whiskey and a bottle of Vodka for Sharla.

The only debt we had left now was a good debt, the mortgage.

"Trust me, not paying interest is worth every penny."

Chapter Thirty

If I can do it… you know…

"If someone has done it, I can do it too. If no one has, then I can be the first." -Soraya

Summer was coming and my car's air conditioning was in need of repairs. The weekend was looking good and the weather even better. We were looking at temperatures of 28 Celsius (82 for you Mare-Kans), with the humidity factor it was going to feel like 36 degrees (96.8 on the Fahrenheit scale). We decided to get it fixed and budgeted $700.00; anything more and it wasn't getting done.

Being new in town (I had been gone for thirty years) I thought I'd go to the shop of a guy I went to school with from grade two to grade eight. Turns out he had no idea who I was. It just goes to show you. To be honest if I hadn't had a crush on his twin sister back in the day, I probably wouldn't have remembered him either.

Anyhow we got to talking and since we lived through some of the same events and had a few friends and old acquaintances in common I got to catch up on people I hadn't seen in over twenty years. We talked about work and I told him that my wife and I had been retired for almost a year.

"Are you the same age as me?" he asked.

"Ya, I'm fifty-three this year." I said.

"You did way better than me." he replied.

I found it odd that he'd say that. After all, I looked around and saw that he had a huge garage with four bays, the building was in a great location and he was booked solid for the foreseeable future. I had called in the morning to book an appointment and was lucky to get in due to a cancellation. From what I could tell he was doing more than fine.

He was happily married, his kids were doing well, he was in the middle of doing some renovations on his house, he went out hunting a couple of times a year, he had a campground he liked to go to and so on and so forth. It looked like he had it all.

So, why did he think that I was doing better than he was? Was it because I was retired? I told him I have friends who work twelve to sixteen hour days and survive on four hours of sleep a night. I had other friends who were full of energy and would be happy to work twenty-four hours a day if they could go without sleep. Turns out, my old classmate had been doing the same thing for about forty years. "I used to love doing this. Now, it's just the same thing, day in and day out. There's no challenge here." he said.

He talked about being exhausted at the end of the day and how there wasn't really any joy in the work anymore. He mentioned having to "do this" for another fifteen years before he could retire. He didn't seem very happy about it. My reflexes kicked in and I started going on about what's important to oneself. I mentioned my Z to A plan and how that worked out for me.

We chatted a little while he worked on my car. When he was done we fist pumped and I told him it was nice to catch up and I left. (I did have to return after two weeks for a check up to make sure all was well.)

As I tend to do, I mulled over our conversation and thought about what he'd said. I got to thinking... What was it that he loved about the work in the past and why didn't he love it anymore? What kind of changes could he make to bring the passion back? I would have loved to have a few sessions with him to talk it over.

Of course there is a good chance that he could retire in the next year or so, if he wanted to. I'm guessing that he probably doesn't have a plan for retirement. Does he even know what his F.I. number (financial independence number) is? I doubt it. How often does he talk with his wife about retirement? What do they want to do? What would their lives look like in the future?

Here's a smart guy with a smart wife. They're running a very successful business making plans, setting appointments and whatnot, yet they have no idea what their retirement is going to look like. He told me his dad retired at sixty-five and he'd do the same.

I went back two weeks later and we chatted a bit more about retirement and making plans. I found over the past few years that it takes a while for people to accept advice or even talk seriously about retirement. When I was working full time and building my path to retirement, most people I worked with didn't understand, didn't care or didn't believe that it was possible. That is until about a month before we left. All of a sudden people were all like, "You're actually doing it? How did you manage it? Why haven't you said anything about it?" Well, they didn't say the last one. I'm sure when my co-workers did an impression of me it was, "Save, save, save. Be debt free. Invest, be smart, don't waste money... blah, blah, blah, I'm going to retire next year."

We all have a tendency to get stuck in our thought paradigms. Times where we don't want to admit we might not know something or that there just might be an alternative way of doing something. The fear of being wrong and not having all the answers can be scary.

Here's something I say almost everyday to myself, "I love being wrong." This doesn't mean that I "like" being wrong. Being wrong can cost me money. It can put a dent in my pride. It can leave me feeling embarrassed, but *rarely* if ever, does it kill me. Mistakes make me stronger, but only if I take the time to look back and see where I went wrong and then learn from them.

I am not the sharpest tool in the shed. I'm not some financial genius. I'm just a guy who created his best worst case scenario, my Z plan and started making tiny little changes. Believe me when I say this, "If I can do it, so can you."

"When you're trying something new and things don't work, don't stop. Just treat it like you treat all the stop signs on the road, just keep rolling and moving forward. I mean if you won't stop for something that could potentially save your life, why would you stop for a small failure?"

Chapter Thirty-One:
Plan L

2017- HELOC

*"Why do banks charge you an NSF fee
(non-sufficient funds fee)
on money they already know you don't have?"*
- Steven Wright

Two years of living without having to pay interest on our credit cards was nice, to say the least. We felt blessed. We were well aware that we were part of the 25% of Canadians who were debt free. It felt so good… and we wanted everyone we knew to experience the feeling.

At this point in our lives everyone in the family was getting an allowance. We were taking our three and four weeks' vacation time in the summer and six weeks of unpaid leave in the winter. We were going to concerts every couple of months and taking mini vacations two or three times a year. It was crazy how far we'd gotten. We often wondered how all this was even possible. It was astonishing how taking tiny little steps could achieve so much. Looking back today I think a big part of it was being grateful for everything we had.

A little side note before I continue.

It's easy to read this and think that our lives were a breeze. Just to be clear, it wasn't. Every March and April around our dead daughter's birthday we suffered with an extended bout of depression. In August the anniversary of her death we suffered from PTSD, our two week "vacation" was anything but that. And just like any parents we had to figure out how to raise our kids. Yes, life often got in the way.

I just want to make sure that you don't think that we lived in some kind of constant euphoric happiness all because we were debt free. There is no way you can always be happy. Nevertheless you can be grateful most of the time and gratefulness leads to a happier life.

And now back to the story…

Yes, we were debt free. Yes, we had over ten weeks of time off a year. Yes, we were on track to retire a few years before we turned sixty-five. Yes, we had good jobs. All the same, we wanted more time off. It seemed that the more time off we had, the more we wanted. It was similar to paying off debt. The more we saw the red ink going down the more we wanted to accelerate the process.

We had taken a two year break from making improvements on plan Z. Like I said, we were pretty happy with what we had achieved. We really wanted to see how early we could retire. How could we take another couple of years off of our retirement date? We figured the fastest way to retirement was getting rid of our mortgage. We understood that we couldn't retire with a mortgage, so plan L would be about paying off the mortgage as quickly as possible. Of course we'd have to do it without spoiling our present lifestyle.

Over the years we'd built up a fair amount of equity in our home and we were now in a position that would allow us to get a HELOC. Before you run out and get one for yourself, know that HELOCs are not for everyone. Actually, I'd say they are not for most people. If you like to spend money and don't care about budgeting, a HELOC is probably not for you. If you're a spender, there's a good chance you could lose your house with a HELOC. That said, if you're a good budgeter, it's probably the best thing you can do to get rid of your mortgage fast.

What's a HELOC? Here's a simplified idea of how a HELOC works. Basically it's a line of credit and every penny you make goes into an account to reduce the balance owing on your mortgage.

For example, if you owed $100,000.00 on your mortgage and your monthly income was $5,000.00, that $5,000.00 would be taken off your mortgage. You would pay interest on $95,000.00. Of course you have to eat and pay bills, therefore you spend say, $2,000.00 for food and stuff. You now owe $97,000.00 on your mortgage and so you pay interest on that balance. The less you spend the more stays on your mortgage. If you're a good budgeter, you'll pay off your mortgage faster because you can put more money on it. Most banks have online calculators you can use. I like the Manulife One calculator myself; it's easy and they have nice clear visuals.

My in-laws were good budgeters and I talked to them about a HELOC. At first they didn't understand the concept, but after explaining it in a few different ways they finally got the idea. It took a couple of years of explaining before they moved over to a HELOC. Like I said before, "If you don't understand what I'm saying… don't do it." This includes your financial advisor's advice. You really need to understand your money and what you are doing with it.

If my in-laws had stayed with their traditional mortgage it would have taken them another fifteen years to pay off their house. With the HELOC they paid it off in five years. They saved thousands and thousands of dollars in interest payments. When we moved to the HELOC, it took us 3 years to pay off our mortgage, saving us 10 years of mortgage payments. Make sure to do your research before jumping into a HELOC. There are fees involved.

I was caught with a little sticker shock when we moved to a HELOC. When we switched over we had about two and a half years left into our five year locked in rate. We had to pay a penalty to get out of our existing mortgage. I'd been raising my "rent" for years now, so when our mortgage company quoted me a fee, it was based on the mortgage payments I was making which was around $600.00 bi-weekly. When I got the final number on the day of closing it was actually $2,000.00 more than what they quoted me. That's because they based the buyout fee on my original $450.00 bi-weekly payment. I was pissed.

It was still worth moving to a HELOC though. We weren't going to lose money, but I'll tell you this, it motivated me to make that money back fast. We first planned on a five to seven year payment schedule. After paying the bank fees, we turned it into a three to five year plan.

"Shoutout to ATM fees for making me buy my own money!" - Anonymous

Chapter Thirty-Two

You need to have a chat with yourself

"Don't be a victim of negative self-talk, remember you're listening." - Bob Proctor

Things aren't always going to go your way. As I'm sure you know, life is full of setbacks. We win, we lose. We fall, we rise. We laugh, we cry. The most important thing we can do for ourselves is to treat ourselves fairly.

On the one hand I find it easy to encourage people and cheer them on. On the other hand, I find it hard to take my own advice. I'm more likely to discourage myself with negative self-talk when things don't go my way. I would never tell someone their dreams are stupid or that they're foolish for trying new things. I wouldn't kick them while they're down or mock them for failing. But when it comes to self-talk, it seems all too easy to bash myself.

Over the last few years I've learned a technique for improving my self-talk. The first thing I do is remind myself that I am the parent to my inner child and I need to talk to myself as a loving parent would talk with their child. The best way I've found to do this is to take two chairs and face them to each other. I sit in one chair as the "child" and I tell the other chair what is going on. When I'm going through a tough time I talk it out as if I'm with a friend. I lay out my fears, my insecurities and whatever problems I have at the time. Once I'm done talking I move to the other chair and respond as a friend or parent would. I try to be encouraging, kind and patient.

When I respond to my inner child I make sure to use my name. This is very important. I know it may sound a little "hippyish" or like mumbo jumbo, but trust me it works. I'll say things like, "Patrick, you're not giving yourself enough credit. Look what you've accomplished by putting your mind to it." or " Pat, here's a list of some of your successes so far." It's so important that you talk to this person and use their name. You're talking to a real person and you need to acknowledge that.

Take time every day to appreciate yourself, to be kind to yourself. If you wouldn't say it to a friend, don't say it to yourself.

"It all begins and ends in the mind. Whatever you give power to,
has power over you, if you allow it." -
Anonymous

Chapter Thirty-Three: Plan K

I'm done and it's only 2019

"I have never liked working. To me, a job is an invasion of privacy. - Anonymous

In September of 2019 Sharla and I were at work getting ready to punch in for our Saturday shift. As we were waiting for the clock to change so that we could scan our card, Sharla looked at me and said, "I'm done. I don't want to do this anymore. Is there any way we can retire next year?"

Retire in 2020, what was she thinking? That was five years ahead of schedule. That's a lot of mortgage payments and investing into our future we'd be losing. I suggested that she retire in January of 2020 and I would continue to work until 2025. I believed that we could still make our early retirement happen with just one of us working.

As it turns out, that's not what she was after. She wanted both of us to retire. "Ok" I said, we'll look at the numbers and see what we can do. For the next couple of weeks we worked on plan K.

We needed to crunch the numbers a few times and work in a multitude of possible life scenarios. This wasn't going to be something that took a day to figure out. This was going to be the biggest life choice we'd ever made. After a few days of talking about it, we decided to do a dry run for one year.

Plan K was about living for a year on $25,000.00. We figured that if we were debt free and had no mortgage we could survive on $25,000.00 a year. It sounded easy enough, but could it be done? All other monies would go straight to the mortgage. If everything worked out as planned by the end of the year we'd only have a few thousand dollars left on the mortgage.

One of the first problems we faced was figuring out how to make up for the five years of money we would have invested in our retirement fund over the next five years.

If we managed to live on $25,000.00 for a year and at the end of it we still wanted to retire by the end of 2020, we'd have to find some more money. After all, that was an extra five years of living without making an income.

We figured we'd be saving about $18,000.00 in interest on the mortgage, so that was a start. We could sell the house and move into a smaller, less expensive place. We'd talked about moving east to be with family when we retired and housing prices were way less there. The profit on the sale of the house would go a long way to making up the lost income.

We could sell our house and use 50% of the funds to buy a new house. The other 50% we'd put into our savings and investments. We set a goal to buy a house, have three years of living expenses in our savings account and put the balance in our TFSA to invest. Things were looking pretty good on paper. Then something happened.

Covid-19. Need I say more?

What a time to be alive. When the pandemic hit we had just started our six weeks leave of absence from work. The government was talking about shut downs and we had no idea what that meant. I remember a friend sending me a video of the line up at Costco. He was standing near the middle of this never ending line that simply disappeared somewhere down the street. I texted a couple of the managers and asked how they were dealing with the situation. It was complete and utter madness. "We're giving out overtime like it's candy," said one of them.

We were so happy to be off work. By day three, we weren't laughing anymore. We could only empathize with the stress all of our co-workers must be under.

We had plans to fly back east to visit family and our flight was canceled. We stayed home on our time off and avoided going shopping for the remainder of the six weeks (except for one food shop). We had no food in the house as we planned on being gone for three weeks. Two weeks before my planned return to work I broke my ankle in two places while on a walk. (how sad is that?) I ended up going back to work with a cast on.

A lot of people were asking us if we'd changed our minds about retiring. The whole world seemed to be falling apart. We told them we pulled out plan Q, of course they had no idea what we were talking about. We told them that we could only control what we could control and that we'd continue on with our plans to retire. If something were to happen, say we couldn't sell our house for example, then we'd stay in town and STOP, DROP and ROLL. In other words, we adjust our plans accordingly.

Over that year we talked with our girls about retirement plans, moving and everything else we wanted to do. We were getting pretty serious about the whole thing. We asked them what they wanted to do. At first they talked about just staying in town and finding a place to live. Over the course of the year they thought about moving back east with us and what that would look like. In the end they ended up moving to Ottawa and finding themselves an apartment. It was nice knowing they were still close to us for a little while longer.

By December of 2020 we realized that the dream was possible. We told our friends that we were going to retire on our wedding anniversary, July 1 2021. No one believed us. We barely believed us. As it turns out, we were a few days off. We retired on July 26.

"For many, retirement is a time for personal growth,
which becomes a path to greater freedom. - Rober Delamontague

Chapter Thirty-five

Don't fear the spider

"Slow breathing is like an anchor in the midst of an emotional storm: the anchor won't make the storm go away, but it will hold you steady until it passes." - Russ Harris

According to US statistics, between four and eleven people a year die from spider bites. Yet 3% to 15% of people suffer from arachnophobia. Using the highest number of deaths from spider bites 11 and using the lowest number of people who suffer with arachnophobia (3%) or 9.8 million Americans, the chances of someone with arachnophobia dying from a spider bite is about 0.0001%.

Why am I telling you this? Am I trying to make people feel bad for having arachnophobia? No. 'Cause I'll be honest, when I see a spider... I call for my wife.

The reason I want to share this little tidbit of information is because I want you to know and remember (and I have to remind myself a lot of the time) that some fears are not based in reality. This is important when working on your Z to A plan. Sure, you can fear the future and come up with worst case scenarios, but you can also come up with solutions and best case scenarios too.

Back in the days when I used to do martial arts, my senseis used to call me the "What-if guy". Why? Because every time they showed us a new move or choke hold or anything, I would always ask, what if. What if I did *this* when you did that? Lucky for me anytime they wanted to hurt someone, I got chosen. The good news is that being the "what if guy" built up my pain tolerance and my skill set.

Why am I telling you this? Because I want you to become a "What if person" too. Come up with problems that you think may come up and find a solution. This way you can build up a set of solutions to whatever ails your retirement plan.

When I talk to people about my Z to A retirement strategy, I get plenty of "what ifs" thrown at me. I don't see it as people trying to discourage me, I see it as an opportunity to share some of my strategies for dealing with those what ifs.

Before we officially removed ourselves from the work world, I had people asking me what I'd do if the market crashed (as it's doing right now in 2022-23). I told them I had three years of living expenses in my savings account. I figured three years should see me through a crash. If it doesn't we'd STOP, DROP and ROLL.

There were a couple of people who asked, "What if the market has a complete collapse and you lose all your money and the banks crash and it doesn't rebound?" To them I said, "If the market collapses and the banks all fold and nothing comes back and we all lose our money, we have much bigger problems in the world than money issues. I probably need to buy a gun to protect myself from the oncoming anarchy. If the collapse hasn't started a world where anarchy is running wild, I'll go get a job and start over."

Others asked what we'd do if we had to go back to work. They said things like, "If you have to go back to work, all this planning would have been a waste of time."

To which I answered, "If I said that you could take three years off work and do whatever it is that you want to do, but at the end of those three years you have to go back to work - you won't be further behind, you'll still have everything you have right now, no debt, no mortgage, just your everyday bills - would you take it? I'm offering you a three year vacation from work where you have full freedom of your time." Often they'd just mumble something about how I wasn't being realistic and they walked away.

My main point is to plan for the worst and hope for the best. Make every letter of your plan count. Point your GPS to the right address and move forward. You know your final destination is retirement or death. All you have to focus on is making small improvements to today's life and your future life. Set your small easy goals, write them down, focus on them, think about them, talk about them, dream about them. Whatever it takes to make an improvement on your Z plan, do it. Don't be afraid to ask for help. Talk to people, get out there and ask for advice from those who've done it or are working on it. Go, go, go.

Whether you like it or not, if you continually try to improve your Z plan, your Z plan will improve. The only thing that can stop you is time or as we say in the business, death.

The journey to your happier, more joy filled life is built with every goal, every dream and every road you're on. It's the life you live while you dream. Live a life that is constantly improving, little by little, step by step. Be as grateful as you can be and help those around you. Don't fear happiness.

Yes, sometimes the shit will hit the fan. Go have a shower and get back to it as soon as you're able.

"Never trust your fears, they don't know your strength." - Athena Singh

Chapter Thirty-Six: Plan J

We're actually doing this and other stories

"Change is hard, but so is staying somewhere you don't belong." - Mandy Hale

In March of 2021 we found ourselves a realtor. We were actually doing it, we were making plans to sell our house. Most of our friends thought we were crazy. We thought we were crazy. "Are we actually doing this?" We asked ourselves more than a few times.

Were we nervous? Of course we were. We had never done anything like this before. Not only were we putting our house up for sale, we were also quitting our jobs. We were giving up a secure living wage and tons of benefits. Saying goodbye to all that money and steady cash flow was a little crazy, but what is life, if it's not one crazy adventure after another?

We had been downsizing during the previous year. As It turns out, that wasn't enough time to get rid of all our crap. We still had tons of stuff to get rid of. What we didn't sell we gave away. By the time June rolled around we were cleaning up and making the place look good for the showings. The house went up on the market and within the first week we had eleven offers. We sold the house, quit our jobs and packed up all of our belongings into the moving truck.

We drove to the ferry terminal and waited for the next ferry to arrive. A few hours later we rolled off the giant boat and that's when things started to feel a little more real. We spent a week driving across the country. We decided to rough it. I slept in the truck and Sharla slept in the car we were towing. We were on the road every morning by 4 am, we'd drive until noon and stop for an hour and a half nap. After that we'd get up and go for a little walk and do some stretching. We'd get back on the road and drive until about an hour before the sun went down.

A week later we arrived in our new home town. We put everything we had into storage and started looking for a new place to call home. As it turns out prices had skyrocketed and every place we looked at was more than we budgeted for and to make this worse every house we looked at had a bidding war.

Although we felt like panicking, we didn't. I'm sure our realtor wasn't very happy with the fact that we were serious about our budget. After about a month we told her we were going to go with our secondary idea. We started looking for a place to rent until things cooled down a little. We explained to our realtor that we didn't suffer from F.O.M.O. (fear of missing out). The last thing we wanted was to buy a house for the sake of buying a house and then have buyer's remorse.

We knew that things weren't always going to go our way and we did the best to plan for the unforeseen. But since the unforeseen is well... unforeseeable you can only plan so much. Lucky for us we had a couple friends who had just finished building a new apartment building and we were able to get in on their last apartment. They asked us if we were interested in the maintenance position that was available, but we graciously turned them down. Even though it was only one day a week of vacuuming the halls, we just weren't interested in being tied down for any reason. We wanted the opportunity to do what we wanted to do, when we wanted to do it. They understood perfectly well.

As it turns out we did end up doing a couple of odd jobs for them. The labor market was pretty tight and they asked us to paint a couple of their older apartments while they were out of town. We told them we'd be happy to help. We offered to do it for free. After all, what are friends for? They refused to let us work for free, and so they put more than a few bucks in our pockets. It was a win/win.

Our plan J was to get a move on, so to speak, and that's just what we did. Renting turned out to be a really good thing. It gave us the opportunity to visit a few towns in the area and check out different neighborhoods. We also discovered the benefits and the drawbacks to apartment/condo living.

After a year of renting, we were ready to move on. We looked at a variety of places in a few different cities. Prices had come down but we still hadn't found a place that suited us. We didn't want to spend another summer in the apartment and so we talked about alternatives. It would have been nice if things had gone as we planned them in our heads, but alas they didn't. So? What were we going to do?

We spent a couple of months throwing out a bunch of ideas. We hadn't really planned on having so many choices available to us. We threw some of our ideas at our friends and family and it just made them dizzy.

We needed a new plan.

"Not knowing is half the fun. The other half is figuring it out."

Chapter Thirty-Seven: Plan I

Now what's going to happen?

"We all make choices, but in the end our choices make us." - Ken Levine

We had so many ideas. Our minds were blasting like fireworks. It was late January 2023 and it was time to get serious about our next plan. We had whittled it down to a hundred and five ideas.

One was to spend the next couple of months downsizing, put everything into storage, buy a motorhome and travel across Canada for the next year.

We'd already done a lot of downsizing before we moved, but we discovered we still had things we were keeping just to have them. For example, I had three hundred vinyl records and the only turntable in my possession was a 1971 Fisher Price music box record player. I emailed a few of the used record stores in town and had multiple offers on my collection. It felt really good to get rid of those records. We decided to continue getting rid of things we really didn't want or need.

Our second idea was to just bite the bullet and buy a house that we were "OK" with and was within our budget. We'd stay put for three to seven years and figure out what comes later.

I know it's a little extreme, but that's what you get with us. The housing market was slowly working into our favor again. Interest rates were going up which put downward pressure on the housing prices and since we were paying cash the uptrend in interest rates was advantageous for us.

We were having such a hard time deciding what to do. We concluded that the only thing that would push us into a decision was to give our notice. We knew if we had a checkered flag we'd be more motivated. Need help making a decision? Give yourself a deadline. That's just what we did.

We decided to put our stuff in storage. If we bought a place we could cancel it, if we went on a cross country trip we'd be ready.

A day after giving our notice serendipity knocked at our door in the form of a text. It was an invitation to spend two months in Mexico with our best man and his wife. Then we got another text asking us if we were planning on visiting the Island soon. When we texted back that we might, our friends told us we could use their secondary house as our home base.

Plan I was coming to life. Spend a year traveling. Who knew? The first thing we did was contact our best man and his wife. Although we'd love to travel with them, Mexico wasn't on our bucket list. We asked if there was any chance that we could stay at their condo in Whistler while they were gone to Mexico. They were more than happy to let us stay there. That was awesome news.

Plan I was a plan to travel across Canada for a year, maybe more, maybe less. We'd head out at the end of April and start by making our way across Ontario. We'd make a stop at my brothers' for a few nights then drive to Niagara Falls for a couple days making a stop in Hamilton to see an old friend. From there we'd make our way to Saskatoon and Edmonton to visit family and friends for a few days. Then we'd drive through the Rockies and make our way to see friends and family on the lower mainland and finally stop for a couple of months at our friends' condo. We figured to be at the condo around the middle of May. Our plan was to stay there until the end of June. Once we left Whistler we'd camp until September.

In September we would move into our friend's secondary house (for a very reasonable price). Since we were planning to be on the Island we decided to call up our old manager at Costco and see if we could work the seasonal period from mid October to December. This would give us an opportunity to visit with all our friends and acquaintances and make a few bucks on the side. Our aim was to use the extra income to pay for a three month trip to Australia where we could visit with Sharla's brother and a couple of old friends. We planned to make our way back in late March early April.

As it turns out we didn't buy a motorhome, we drove our car. By the way, we should have gotten a motorhome. Oh well. As of this writing, I'm sitting in my buddy's condo in Whistler. We're going for hikes every day and we're feeling totally blessed for all the opportunities so far.

There is just no way that when we built our original Z plan we would've dreamed of this kind of scenario. We thought by the time we reached our K plan that we'd be in our new home working and playing in our backyard. This is the beauty of going with the flow.

To be honest, it's not like things were as easy as writing about them. I mean, before we took off we had tons to do and the stress levels were pretty high. But that's what happens when you try something new. We would take time everyday to remind ourselves of what we were doing and we made our "get things done" list.

We're sure that we will encounter a few bumps in the road and we're pretty sure some things in our travel plans will change here and there. We'll do what we usually do, we'll pivot and change.

"Enjoy life while it is happening." - Richard L. Evans

Chapter Thirty-Eight

It's not you… it's them

"It is better to be hated for what you are,
then to be loved for what you are not."
- André Gide

There will come a time when you feel comfortable talking about your dreams of becoming debt free, starting your own side hustle, retiring or whatever your dreams are. When you do, be ready for the haters, the doubters and the discouragers. They won't just disappear.

The Haters

The people you simply don't want or need in your life. I know it sounds bold and harsh, but it's true. If someone is discouraging you and bringing you down and talking shit about you… why would you want that kind of person in your life? These are the easiest people to get rid of. Yes, they'll talk bad about you after you leave them, but in the end it'll be worth it. Look, we all have enough problems dealing with our own negative self-talk and imposter syndrome; we don't need people piling on the shit, we need people willing to shovel some of it off of us.

But before you start cutting people out of your life you'll want to sit with them and have a chat. Tell them that you are working on improving your situation and that you would appreciate it if they could help you by being encouraging and supportive of your new goals. They don't have to agree or even believe in you. You are simply asking them as a friend to be supportive. Maybe even ask them if they want to join you on the adventure as they create their own goals and plans.

Let them know that their support and encouragement will be appreciated and welcomed. Be honest and tell them you are just like everyone else. You have fears about doing something new and going into the unknown. Sure you're afraid to fail, but you've come to understand that Failure x Repetition = Success and the more you fail the less you're afraid of it. Fill them in on the fact that it will be much easier to get over a failure if they are by your side helping you get back on your feet.

If you find that after a few days or weeks that certain people just can't manage to be supportive, it may be time to cut the cord. That's not to say they will never come back into your life. Maybe one day they'll see the light and become a true friend. There may be a time when they come to you and ask you to help them and mentor them.

Until then, you need to delete them from your life. Harsh as that may be. Remember these are the true haters in your life. People who actually fear you climbing up and making your life more positive. These people will hold you down because they feel it's better to hold you down at their level then to be left alone.

The Doubters

These folks are the people who know you and judge you by your past actions. They probably see you as a dreamer, who never achieved any of their dreams. These people love you and don't want to see you get hurt. They believe that Failure = Defeat.

They don't understand that you see failure as an opportunity to learn and move forward. As Thomas A. Edison famously said, "I have not failed. I've just found 10,000 ways that won't work." You too are starting to think that way. On purpose and with purpose.

More often than not the doubters in your life aren't bad people, they're just stuck in a negative mindset. Some people would say that you have to rid yourself of these people too, but most of the time this type of person is probably a family member or a long time friend. It's not that they don't believe in you, it's that they don't believe that *you* believe in you.

It took me a long time to realize that the doubters in my life weren't against me, it's just that they were stuck in their own thought paradigm of who they thought I was or what I should be. Every time I failed they saw it as a singular failure, one more thing to add to the heap. They didn't understand that I was learning from those failures and I was ok with failing. To be honest the hardest part was trying to explain why I was ok with failing. I often wondered if maybe I was crazy for thinking this way. I didn't grow up with anyone who thought like me.

Growing up in low income housing where ninety percent of homes were fatherless, it was hard for a boy like me to find a father figure to look up to. Most of us just looked up to the oldest boy we knew. Needless to say most eighteen to twenty year olds weren't trying to set any kind of fatherly example.

I was one of the lucky few. When I was about twelve years old my mom started dating a man twenty years her senior. Gerry became the father I never had. He'd owned multiple businesses, his kids were university graduates and business owners. This man never uttered a discouraging word. Any time I had a crazy idea, everyone around me would laugh at me and tell me to stop being such a dreamer. But Gerry never discouraged me, he would always ask "how", "*How* are you going to do it?"

To be honest, I never really understood the power of his words until I was in my late twenties. His "How?" wasn't there to discourage me but to challenge me. He was helping me figure out how to get what I wanted. It also made me think about whether I really wanted it. A lot of times I was just daydreaming and brainstorming. There is no way I could ever do everything I think of… sometimes it was just fun talking about it like I was going to do it. I was really blessed to have one strong voice of encouragement in my corner.

The important thing when dealing with your doubters is repetition. Help them understand that you see failure as a stepping stone. Tell them that you are encouraged by Edison's quote, "When you have exhausted all possibilities, remember this - you haven't."

The sad reality is some people will always be doubters, but that's on them, not you. Don't let it bring you down. Let them know that you believe in you and that's the most important thing.

It's funny how even now, I still have people in my life who think that I'm too much of a dreamer. If I were to be totally honest about it, I'd have to admit that it does kinda hurt that some people are just waiting for the other shoe to drop; they're still seeing "me" in their old paradigm. They just can't seem to shake the old me out of their minds. Others think that there is no way that my lifestyle is sustainable. At some point I'll be broke and will have to return to work and they tell me I'll be worse off than I was before.

I try to point out to them that I've thought it through pretty hard. I have come up with worst case scenarios. Maybe one day I will have to return to the work world (for whatever reason). But I don't dwell on the "what-ifs." I'm just trying to live my best life right now and right now has enough in it to keep me busy. I'm not afraid to go back to work. If I want something that is not in my life budget, let's say a trip to Australia for example, I'll go to work and make enough money to pay for it. Otherwise I won't go. Working for what you want is not a failure.

Right now I have all this free time and I'm taking advantage of it. The fact that I did it once only means that I can do it again. Still they can't seem to wrap their minds around it. After all, it's just, little old me. How could I possibly have solved a problem as big as enjoying one's life?

To that I say, "If I can do it, so can you."

The Discouragers who love you.

We all know people like this, but in my opinion, I think "The Discouragers who love you" are often misunderstood. I'll give you a personal example.

My mom - if there was anyone in my life that could put the kibosh in my dreams, it was her. Yes, my mom was an expert dream killer.

"Mom, I want to be an Olympic diver." I said to her when I was twelve.

"Stop dreaming in color, I'm broke with five kids and you think you're going to the Olympics? That's never going to happen."

Another time I told her I wanted to be a stand up comedian. She said I'd never do it. I told her I had a time slot booked for the next night. She said, "But you're not funny. Comedians make people laugh. What are you going to do? And who told you, you were funny?"

You get the idea. It didn't matter what success I had under my belt. The next thing I attempted was sure to fail.

Just to be clear, I love my mom. I call her almost every night and I go see her as often as I can. So, what is her problem?

Well, what if I told you my mom was born in 1940, in a village of two thousand people? When she was in grade three, she had to quit school to help take care of her siblings. Her mom died giving birth to her fourteenth child, when my mom was only five years old. In the summer of her tenth year, one of her brothers drowned and another died of food poisoning after eating wild mushrooms. She left home at twelve and got a job at a local store where she tended the store and took care of the owner's children and received room and board as her pay. When she was around seventeen, she had to get all her teeth removed. She saved up for a few years and was able to buy herself dentures.

On and on her story goes. She worked for a butcher, cleaning houses, sewing… She met my dad and had five kids. My father left her with a nine month old, a three year old, a six, seven and eight year old. I think you get it.

Was my mom being mean to me with her discouraging words? Nope. She was trying to help in the best way possible. She didn't want me to fail, she didn't want me to get hurt. Life is hard and cruel and your only dream should be to get a job, have a roof over your head and eat. Survival is your goal.

I always tell my kids, make lots of mistakes before you're twenty-five, because they don't really matter. Once in a while they'll tell me they want to try something and my first instinct is to discourage them. Not because I don't think they can do it, but because I want to protect them from making mistakes and getting hurt. Once I get over my own fear, I do my best to encourage them.

I guess my takeaway on "The Discouragers" is:

1. They've lived their lives in fear of being too happy. They believe if you're too happy something really bad is going to happen to you. Karma wants to bring you down a notch.
2. They don't want to see you get hurt. They just want you to play it safe. Get a job, pay your bills and try not to amass too much debt.

Be gentle on the "Discouragers who love you", keep explaining to them that you don't see failure as an end. You see failure as a way not to do something, which in turn is a success. As strange as that sounds.

"Haters will see you walk on water and say it's because you can't swim." – Anonymous

Chapter Thirty-Nine

We are not the same

"Your life isn't yours if you constantly care what others think of you." - Anonymous

I've said it before and I'll say it again. "We are not the same."

There are no two retirement plans that are going to be identical. Sure they may have some similarities, but in the end it's your life, it's your retirement, it's your plan. The goal of this book has never been to get you to some magical-one-size-fits-all retirement. It's about looking at where your life is headed right now. It's about knowing what your Z plan is and then see how you can improve on that plan.

You'll need to understand what your motivators are. Are you an 80% time, 10% money, 10% toys kind of a person? What's your combo? Look back on your life and find times where you were really happy, what were you doing? Were you working sixty hours a week, making tons of money and loving every minute of it? Or, were you sitting on a swing in the backyard reading a book?

Keep in mind that although money in and of itself will not bring you joy, you will need a certain amount of it to achieve your financial independence. Yes, you will need money to retire and yes, you will need to know how to manage that money so that you can stay retired and enjoy the life you want. Your goal should be to keep moving towards the life you dream of.

"You are you and that's the only thing you really need to know to start truly living your life."

Chapter Forty

A short story…

"Making someone responsible for your misery also makes them responsible for your happiness. Why give that power to anyone but yourself?"

- Scott Stabile

There was this couple… Mr. and Mrs. Kynoreel, a wonderful couple who loved to laugh and play. Mr. Kynoreel was the kind of guy who laughed at every joke, yet couldn't seem to tell one. He was a super friendly person who was always ready to chat with everyone all the time.

One day a minimum wage couple were invited to a small gathering at the Kynoreels. As they took their first step into the house, they let out a gasp. The entrance had twenty-five foot ceilings and a double staircase led to a large open hallway-like balcony. It was a six thousand square foot palace of awe.

The minimum wage couple's first thought was, we want to be this rich one day. We want to be as happy as the Kynoreels. These people had it all, a successful business, a wonderful family, a couple of nice cars, tons of friends and the list went on and on.

What the minimum wage couple didn't know was that the Kynoreels were on the verge of bankruptcy. Mr. Kynoreel was completely stressed out and was suffering from depression. Within a few weeks he'd be having a nervous breakdown. Within a few months they would lose their house, the cars and almost lose their business.

Years later, a random chance would bring the two couples back together. The minimum wage couple had just started working on their Z to A plan and would discover that not long after they'd met, Mr. Kynoreel basically had to start everything over from scratch. He had moved his family into a small apartment and started his business all over again. After two years of hard work, they were able to buy a house and were once again working their way back to the top.

A couple of more years passed and they met up again. The minimum wage couple had now been working on their Z to A plan for a few years and found themselves in a great position in life. The Kynoreels on the other hand were having a really hard time, it seems they found it difficult staying out of debt. Apparently keeping up with the Joneses came at a heavy cost.

You see, the Kynoreels were just like those tailgaters on the highway. The drivers who need to pass you and when they do, they need to pass the next person. They look forward to that moment when they'll finally be the lead car with no one in front of them to slow them down. What they don't seem to realize is that there is always another car somewhere in the distance.

At this meeting point the Kynoreels were coming back from a financial seminar where they'd learned about budgeting, financial responsibility and how to get out of debt. The minimum wage couple found it very interesting until they found out that the seminar cost $2,500.00 per person and they had just flown to Vegas to go see it.

Mr. Minimum wage was slightly confused and blurted out, "So, let me get this straight. You're in debt over your head and you just spent $5,000.00 to go to a seminar about being financially responsible? *And…* You don't see the irony?"

"Oh no," they said in unison. "This seminar has changed our lives. It was so eye opening that we're flying to Arizona next month to go see it again. You should come with us."

At this point the minimum wage couple were a few years into retirement planning and let the Kynoreels know that they were on track to achieve financial independence by the time they were fifty-nine.

"How is that possible?" Mr. Kynoreel asked. "Don't you just work nine-to-five jobs?"

The minimum wage couple explained the many ways they had learned to be more financially responsible. They talked about their Z plan and how every tiny step they took led to improving their future and their present. They told the Kynoreels that they'd be happy to offer them some advice and share what they had learned and what had worked for them.

"You know what they say," said Mr. Kynoreel, "free advice is worth just that, nothing." Last they heard Mr. and Mrs. Kynoreel were divorced. Mr. Kynoreel still travels all over the place making sure he looks rich and happy.

It seemed that Mr. and Mrs. Kynoreel thought that happiness was just passing the next car on the road. If only they could pass this next car, then they'd be happy. But sadly they discover there's another car in front of them, and so they must pass that one to finally be happy and so on and so on.

Are the Kynoreels bad people? Absolutely not. They are wonderful people who are ready to help their friends at a moment's notice. They are loving, kind and considerate. Their biggest problem is that they're constantly reaching for something they'll never get. The irony is that if they stopped for a moment, they'd see that happiness is within their grasp.

If only they got in the slow lane and put their car in cruise control, they might realize that the trip itself is where happiness lies.

"Whenever you find yourself on the side of the majority, it is time to pause and reflect."

- Mark Twain

Chapter Forty-one

Look at it this way

"Looking at life from a different perspective makes you realize that it's not the deer that is crossing the road, rather it's the road that is crossing the forest." -Muhammad Ali

The whole is greater than the sum of its parts. Another way of saying this is that things are better together than alone. The human body is made up of oxygen, carbon, hydrogen, nitrogen, calcium, sulfur and the list goes on… Individually none of these things can think, create art, write or love. Apart they are not self aware, yet, when they come together in the right amounts… there you are.

What does that have to do with your Z plan? A lot. Think of your retirement as the "WHOLE" and the steps you take to get there as the "SUM OF ITS PARTS". You know that putting one payment on your credit card and reducing your balance by $5.00 (a part) is not in and of itself going to magically put you in a position to retire (the whole). For that matter, neither is putting $10.00 into your RRSP (a part), going to do it either.

But after years of making those small payments and investments, you'll be able to look back and see what the sum of all those tiny parts turned into. It's like going to the gym. You won't notice anything new after one or two workouts, but I guarantee if you show up to the gym day in and day out… one day you'll look in the mirror and see something new. All those tiny steps will make a difference.

We need to look at debt, investing, happiness, retirement and life from a different perspective. Sometimes we need to focus on the whole and other times the parts. It's never just one or the other. Now and then we may get intimidated by the largeness of the dream. The road may seem too long and impossible to traverse. When those days come, and they will, look at the sum of its parts. Think back to your accomplishments and remind yourself of all the tiny steps it took to achieve the results you now have.

There are times when I'm struggling with my dreams, times when I'm suffering from imposter syndrome. I think maybe I just got lucky up to this moment and perhaps my luck has run out. I find it difficult to pull myself out of a rut when things start to pile up on top of me.

Deep inside, I know I can overcome whatever it is I'm going through. I just have to set the dominos in motion. The first thing I do is accept the situation. It is what it is. Now what? I try to come up with a logical way to overcome the situation. If I have to be totally honest, that rarely works. So what do I do? I move on to step two, I look for solutions that are out of the ordinary. I brainstorm, I dream, I imagine ridiculous fixes and resolutions to my problems. There are times when my wife and I contrive the craziest of ideas, so much so that they make us laugh out loud. That's usually when we realize things aren't as bad as we think. That rut is not as deep and as wide as it first appeared. We just had to get out and look at it from a different angle. After that we return to step one and we mix a little logic in with all that craziness.

Whatever problems you are facing, be it debt, investing, housing, family problems… *add your problem here*, take a moment and try to clear your mind. Break the problem down into tiny chewable pieces. Look at it from different angles. Use the two chair system. Sit down and pretend that a friend is asking you to help them with this exact problem. What kind of advice would you give your friend?

Oftentimes inviting a friend or two over and hashing out a few ideas will go a long way. It can help you see that all is not lost. Maybe one of your friends has gone through what you are going through and has a simple solution. The important thing is to break it down into manageable pieces, then break those pieces down a little too and go from there.

"The happiness of your life depends upon the quality of your thoughts."
- Marcus Aurelius

Chapter forty two

Car stories

"I couldn't repair your brakes, so I made your horn louder."

- Anonymous

The following car stories are nothing more than that.

Let me tell you about our 2017 Chevy Sonic. What a great little car. In one of the previous chapters I probably talked about our pickup truck, well… After we got rid of the truck we picked up a 1997 Sunfire as our second car. (remember the new driver in the family?) At the time our daughter was learning to drive we had a 2005 Chevy Cavalier with a stick shift. I'll tell you the story of that car first (unless you're too busy to hear it?).

In February of 2006, we'd been in our new house for about seven months and I had been working at Costco for about five months. I was making about $2 above minimum wage and was still working part-time. Anyhow, my backyard neighbor Don asked me if I wanted to buy his car.

"Hey! Pat, you wanna buy my car?" he shouted over the fence.

"What kind of car is it?" I asked.

"It's a 2005 Chevy Cavalier. Uh, do you know how to drive a standard?" he responded.

"I love driving standards, but that's a brand new car. How much did you pay for it?"

"I paid $13,000.00 for it and I just made the final payment on it last month."

"Impressive. You paid your car off in one year. But sorry dude." was my reply. "I just started working part-time at Costco and there is no way I can afford a new car. I'm barely making ends meet right now as it is."

"Tell you what." he said to me. "I'll sell it to you for $4,500.00."

"What? What's wrong with it?" I was surprised by the price.

"Nothing," he said. "It's got mostly highway miles on it and runs like a charm."

"Why are you selling it?"

A big grin covered his face. "I just won a brand new fifty thousand dollar SUV through the hospital lottery. I figured since the Cavalier is paid off, why not share the luck?"

"Let me see what I can do." I said, "I'd hate to turn down a deal like that."

"Take your time. I won't sell it to anyone until you let me know what you want to do."

My daughters had recently each received a thousand dollar inheritance from their great-grand-father. I borrowed the money and set up a repayment schedule at a ten percent interest rate. I preferred to pay them interest instead of the banks. I told Don I'd secured $2000.00 cash and wondered if he'd let me pay off the rest in a few installments. He agreed and soon we were driving home our brand new car.

At the time we owned a 1987 Oldsmobile that had been given to us by Sharla's parents. They received the car from Sharla's Great Uncle Lloyd. It was running pretty rough but still had some life left in her, so I gave it to a girl I knew who was going to university. I think she got a couple of years out of it.

As for the Cavalier, that car was the best thing we ever bought. The only money I ever put into it was four tires, a battery and regular oil changes. We ended up selling it the summer before we moved. I sold it for $357.65 to a family who was in need of a car. Why that price exactly? It was one month's worth of interest on our mortgage at the time. I don't know why… I just do things like that.

A couple of years before we retired we decided to buy a newer car and become a one car couple. We bought a Chevy Sonic. Since we still had the Cavalier we weren't in a rush to buy a newer car. That said, we were in the market. We had saved up $11,500.00 in cash to buy a second car. We looked around and I did tons of research over the next few months. One day we thought we'd pop by a couple of dealerships just to see what was available. My eye caught this nice little 2015 Chevy Sonic. I went home, did some research and found that this car, year, make and model had almost no issues with it. The biggest problem I found was the air conditioner compressor went on them. Turns out I had to have that fixed in 2022.

The dealer wanted $17,500.00 plus taxes, plus "administration" fees for it, which wasn't a bad deal since the car was only two years old, and came with all the bells and whistles. Brand new the car retailed at just over $22,000.00 plus taxes and fees. The first thing the salesman told me was that the car was from another province. That's not a big problem for me, but I know that for most people who are buying a car, a thing like that will scare them off.

I asked how long the car had been on the lot and was told just shy of a month. I made an offer of $11,500.00 all in. He shook his head in disappointment. "That's not realistic. I might be able to do $17,200.00 plus taxes and fees" he said.

"Oh, I see. You think I'm trying to negotiate. I get it. Here's the deal." I said, "I have $11,500.00 cash, not a penny more."

He told me there was no way he could let it go for that, but he could show me something in that price range. I told him that I had walked the lot and the only thing I could see spending my money on was that car. I thanked him for his ten minutes and told him I'd be back in a couple of weeks to see if the car was still available.

Two weeks later I came back and the car was still there. This time it was marked down by about a thousand bucks. I went in and found the guy I'd talked to a couple of weeks earlier. He turned my offer down again. I told him I'd be back in a couple of weeks.

I figured that since the car was from out of province there was a really good chance it wasn't going to sell and since I wasn't in a rush, I took my chances. I went in a few weeks later and the car had been marked down to $14,900.00. By this time that car had been on the lot for close to 90 days and I had a feeling that in a few days it would be on its way to the wholesale auction.

I walked in and found the man I was looking for. We sat down and I told him what he already knew. The car would be on its way to the wholesale auction in a matter of days. I bluffed a little when I told him an out of province car like that might fetch $8,500.00 at an auction. I offered him $11,500.00. "Hold on a minute, I have to go talk to my boss," he said.
"Do what you have to do." I replied.

He came back a few minutes later and told me that they had put a protective undercoat on the car and that was $350.00 and that I would have to pay tax and fees on top of the $11,500.00 that I offered him.

I smiled and I might have seemed a little passive aggressive at the time, but let's be honest I'd been there four times already. I said, "Listen Mike, I have $11,500.00 cash on me. You can do whatever you want to that car, undercoat it, paint it, put new tires on it, whatever. But I am not spending a penny more than what I've offered."

He shook his head and said no deal. I'll be honest, I was disappointed. But that was my budget. I got up and started making my way to the door. By the time I hit the door he called me back. We made the deal and I drove away in my new $11,500.00 car (all in).

I know it may seem like I'm a bit of a dick, but it's my money. I worked hard for it and I knew the true value of the car (my true value) and my patience paid off. If I had been desperate, I probably would have paid full price the first time around. The lesson here is be prepared and be patient.

Those are my car stories for now.

"A dream without ambition is like a car without gas, you're not going anywhere."
-Anonymous

Chapter Forty three
Thanks for popping by

"When the story is good, the ending always comes too soon."

-K Tolnoe

Well, I hope you've had fun reading this book. My main ambition was to try to encourage you in making small changes in your life. I know I talked a lot about finances, but the lessons I've learned and tried to impart to you are practical for all parts of life. Tiny steps can improve your marriage, they can make you a better parent, a friendlier friend or a better budgeter. Go out there and make small changes in your life and the lives of those you encounter.

One more story for the road…

One day my friend Peter and I were having a chat about retirement and he asked me, "What does retirement look like for you?"

I was confused by the question. At this point in my life my goal was to retire at fifty-seven or better and I thought I was doing pretty good. For some reason I still had that need to have a networth of a million dollars to retire. So I said, "A million dollars."

Peter looked a little confused, "That's a number. How do you know it's enough? How do you know that you don't need more or less?"

His comment stumped me, "What are you talking about Peter?"

He continued… "When you're retired, you wake up in the morning and then what happens? How do you spend your day? What are you doing? Are you playing in your backyard or are you traveling around the world? Playing in your backyard is way cheaper than traveling around the world. There is no way that you can truely and safely retire if you don't know how much it's going to cost you."

My mind was blown. I mean we had plans to retire by the time we were fifty-seven, but we never really thought about the actual long term cost of retiring. We figured we'd save up as much as possible and then make ends meet. We were good at budgeting and we reasoned that we'd make it work. When we started counting the cost of our retirement and the things we wanted out of life, we realized we were almost there. We could probably retire by the time we were fifty-five and as you know, we actually retired at fifty-two.

I was pretty cocky with some of my self-talk at times. You know, you're doing pretty good and things are going smoothly and I thought I knew everything… or at least enough. But then Peter with just a few words of advice changed my Z plan and cut a few years off our timeline. Think about it. No exchange of money was made. There was no real plan to work out. All Peter did was ask me a question and it made me look at all my savings, investments and future plans in a different way. It was just another tiny little thing that changed my life. Never stop seeking advice from smart people. Thank you Peter.

It's been fun… There's really not much more to say. I just want you to remember a few things.

1. Think of your future self.
2. Remind yourself that Failure x Repetition = Success.
3. And Failure x Repetition is Success.
4. All you have to do is take a tiny little step forward every day (no matter how small).
5. Do it now!
6. "If you cannot do great things, do small things in a great way." – Napoleon Hill
7. It's not always going to be this hard and it's not always going to be this easy.
8. Remind yourself of what you are going for... everyday.
9. Build your emergency fund over time.
10. Help others to achieve their goals and you'll achieve yours.

"In the end, we'll all become stories."

- Margaret Atwood